P9-APJ-387

ICELAND

Eygló Svala Arnarsdóttir, Egill Bjarnason, Jeannie Riley,
Zoë Robert, Þorgnýr Thoroddsen

View over Vík with the sea stacks of Reynisfjara in the distance (p122)

SKIES
ALIGHT

Green, pink, purple, red, white and even yellow Northern Lights (aurora borealis) can be seen dancing across clear dark skies. The colourful winter late morning sunrises and early sunsets are also a spectacle. If you're visiting during the bright summers, stay up to watch the midnight sun barely set – and then rise again – or make the most of the long days and go for an evening hike.

→ CELESTIAL OFFERINGS

The Northern Lights get all the attention, but they share the sky with bright stars, meteor showers and the midnight sun.

▶ Learn more on p176 and p178

Left Northern Lights, Jökulsárlón glacier lagoon **Right** The Milky Way **Below** Summer sunset captured near Reykjavik

ENDLESS DAYS

In midsummer, the earth is more tilted towards the sun resulting in 24-hour daylight in parts of Iceland. The further north you go, the brighter the nights.

↑ LIGHT & DARK

Some visitors find the long days disorienting. The bright nights can interfere with your sleep, so bring an eye mask in case you're camping or on the off-chance your accommodation doesn't have blackout curtains. Likewise, the long winter days can make you feel sluggish. Locals take vitamin D–rich cod-liver oil to compensate for the lack of light.

Best Viewing Experiences

▶ Go in search of the Northern Lights along the Arctic Coast Way. (p174)

▶ Gaze up at the stars and spot the constellations. (p178)

▶ Summit Snæfellsjökull glacier on a midnight-sun hike. (p220)

▶ Celebrate the summer solstice on Grímsey island on the Arctic Circle. (p190)

▶ Kayak along the coast off Grundarfjörður for views of Kirkjufell mountain in the summer evening light. (p224)

ARTS &
HERITAGE

Culture and history buffs visiting Iceland won't be disappointed. Festivals and concerts are held around the country, and beyond the grand galleries in Reykjavík, there are quirky little museums in even the smallest of settlements. Unique ways to immerse yourself in the sagas await, like taking a dip in Grettislaug pool and going to battle via a virtual reality exhibition.

Left Turf houses at the museum at Laufás **Right** Statue of Leifur Eiríksson, Reykjavík **Below** Reykjavík Art Museum, Hafnarhús

→ VIKING
DISCOVERIES

According to the sagas, Leifur Eiríksson arrived in America 500 years before Columbus.

▶ Learn more about the Norse explorers on p227

IN FOCUS

Scenes from a number of blockbusters and popular TV series have been shot in Iceland, including *Game of Thrones, Eurovision Song Contest: The Story of Fire Saga, Fast & Furious 8* and *Rogue One: A Star Wars Story.*

▶ Read about filming locations on p188

↑ MUST VISIT

The Reykjavík Art Museum, hosted at three locations and exhibiting local and international modern and contemporary artists, is a real gem. The museum also houses the collections of three of Iceland's most famous artists: Erró, Jóhannes Kjarval and Ásmundur Sveinsson.

▶ Find out more on p71

Best History & Culture Experiences

▶ Visit the Alþingi, site of Iceland's first parliament in 930 CE. (p86)

▶ Share the festive spirit on Reykjavík Culture Night. (p66)

▶ Explore saga sites and hear stories of settlement in history-rich West Iceland. (p226)

▶ Observe curious exhibitions at the Icelandic Folk and Outsider Art Museum outside Akureyri. (p164)

▶ Become a warrior and take part in a virtual reality Battle of Iceland. (p187)

HOT-WATER
HEALING

Icelanders have been harnessing the power of geothermal heat for centuries. Today, almost every town has a heated swimming pool with hot-pots, and a regular visit – no matter the weather – is very much part of local culture. More recently, spas and geothermal baths have been popping up in stunning locations all over the country, offering next-level luxury. Visiting natural hot springs, however, remains a unique experience.

→ SPA VS SPRING

Spa lovers are spoilt for choice with baths overlooking the ocean, lakes and mountains. But the no-fuss natural hot springs remain authentic and free.

▶ Discover more on p197, p207 and p233

Left Natural hot springs, Landmannalaugar **Right** Blue Lagoon **Below** Sea swimming near Reykjavík

POOL ETIQUETTE

To maintain hygiene and keep chlorine levels low, pool guests must first shower naked. Communal showering is part of the pool culture, so do your best to fit in.

▶ Learn about correct etiquette on p104

↑ NEW BEGINNINGS

Sea swimming exploded in popularity during Covid-19. Join the annual New Year's Day dip at Nauthólsvík, followed by a catch-up in the hot tub.

▶ Read more on p29

Best Soaking Experiences

▶ Submerge in the milky-blue water of the Blue Lagoon and find out what all the hype is about. (p102)

▶ Discover natural hot springs and pools in unforgettable settings along the Westfjords Way. (p207)

▶ Follow the 7-Step Ritual at the newly opened Sky Lagoon. (p107)

▶ Do as locals do and sweat it out in the steam room at the local swimming pool. (p107)

▶ Gaze out onto the fjord from Hofsós pool. (p181)

CULINARY
DELIGHTS

Eating out in Iceland certainly isn't cheap, but choose wisely and you may end up enjoying some of the best food experiences of your life. Innovative chefs are spotlighting local ingredients and modernising traditional cuisine into a feast on all fronts. Seafood and lamb feature heavily, but vegetarian and vegan options are widely available.

→ **FROZEN FAVOURITE**

Icelanders love ice cream, even on the coldest of days. Ice-cream parlours are all over the country. For something fancy, try Omnom in Reykjavík.

Left Langoustines on salad **Right** Ice cream **Below** People gather around a beachside picnic table

MUST TRY

A family-run restaurant on Vestmannaeyjar, Slippurinn uses only local produce and follows the philosophies of New Nordic and Slow Food.

▶ Read about Vestmannaeyjar on p114

↑ **PACK A PICNIC**

Prepare your favourite snacks, find a bench or throw out a blanket and dine in nature.

Best Food Experiences

▶ **Dine at some of Reykjavík's top-notch eateries.** (p52)

▶ **Savour hyper-local flavours on a trip to Flatey island in Breiðafjörður.** (p225)

▶ **Catch your own fish off the North Iceland village of Hauganes.** (p180)

▶ **Taste the increasing selection of local craft beers.** (p64)

▶ **Treat yourself to some 'Icelandic lobster', a speciality of the town of Höfn.** (p155)

HIDDEN
WONDERS

████ While checking off your list of big attractions, keep an eye out for unexpected discoveries. Beyond the top sites are lesser-known gems worth the extra mile. Ask locals for tips as you travel around the island. If you're lucky, they might share some of their secrets – or you'll uncover your own!

→ **QUIET NEIGHBOUR**

Want a tip for another spectacular waterfall? Kvernufoss is a must-visit, hidden not far from its more famous neighbour, Skógafoss.

▶ Read about the falls on p121

Left Spectacular Stórurð valley **Right** Kvernufoss **Below** Remote Flatey Island, North Iceland

←**ROCK & WATER**

Accessible on a day hike, the vibrant blue-green lagoon at Stórurð is surrounded by giant boulders and sits atop a mountain ridge in East Iceland.

▶ Learn more about Stórurð on p153

↑ **ESCAPE INTO TIMELESSNESS**

Just like the West Iceland island of the same name, the Flatey of the north seems light years away from the busyness of modern daily life.

▶ Discover this private paradise on p191

Best Surprise Experiences

▶ **Drive the Arctic Coast Way, passing oceanic vistas, remote natural gems and coastal villages.** (p180)

▶ **Walk through Iceland's largest forest at Hallormsstaður.** (p150)

▶ **Uncover the Eastfjords' artist hub of Seyðisfjörður.** (p145)

▶ **Photograph tucked-away waterfalls along the South Coast.** (p120)

▶ **Paddle to Vigur island, a birdwatcher's paradise.** (p203)

FIRE
& ICE

It's hard to avoid the fire and ice cliché because it describes Iceland's geology so well. Glaciers cover around 10% of the area of the country and volcanic activity is a fact of life. The lava flows from the recent Fagradalsfjall eruption exemplify the island's everchanging landscape. Even post-eruption, the site will be an interesting one to visit.

→ THE BIG MELT

Iceland's glaciers have been rapidly retreating. At risk of disappearing by mid-century, Snæfellsjökull is a reminder of what the planet stands to lose due to climate change.

▶ Learn more about Snæfellsjökull on p220

Left Volcanic crater lava, Reykjanes Peninsula **Right** Snæfellsjökull **Below** Snorkellers explore a crack fissure drift, Þingvellir National Park

LAVA LAND

Spend a couple of hours walking around Berserkjahraun. The moss-covered lava field on Snæfellsnes is a world of its own

▶ See this wonder of Snæfellsnes on p223

↑ TOP EXPERIENCE

When visiting Þingvellir National Park, dive where the two continents meet.

▶ Discover Þingvellir on p86

Best Active Experiences

▶ **Hike towards Fagradalsfjall to witness the site of Iceland's 2021 eruption.** (p108)

▶ **Descend into the dormant volcano of Þríhnúkagígur to a depth of 213m.** (p109)

▶ **Explore an ice tunnel in Langjökull glacier.** (p232)

▶ **Visit Heimaey island in Vestmannaeyjar, evacuated – and since resettled – during the 1973 eruption.** (p114)

▶ **Ski Snæfellsjökull, the 1446m glacier-topped stratovolcano on Snæfellsnes Peninsula.** (p220)

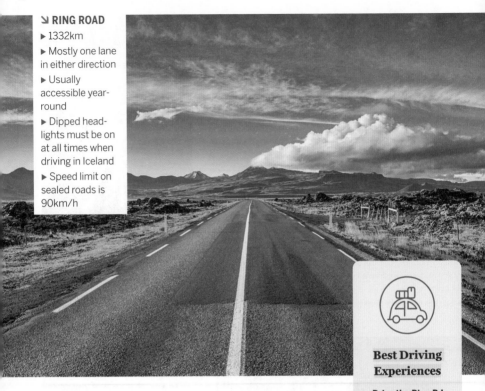

↘ **RING ROAD**

▸ 1332km

▸ Mostly one lane in either direction

▸ Usually accessible year-round

▸ Dipped head-lights must be on at all times when driving in Iceland

▸ Speed limit on sealed roads is 90km/h

EPIC
ROAD TRIP

▬▬ Iceland's Ring Rd (Rte 1; pictured) encircles the island, connecting most of its inhabited regions. A road trip along the 1332km national highway takes you past jagged coastline, secluded fishing villages, glistening glaciers and waterfall after dazzling waterfall. There are plenty of options for detours along the way too.

Best Driving Experiences

▸ **Drive the Ring Rd between Reykjavík and Vík, passing waterfalls, glaciers and black beaches.** (p122)

▸ **Continue past Vík along the south coast to Jökulsárlón for its iceberg-filled lagoon.** (p140)

▸ **Check out the Arctic Coast Way and Westfjords Way.** (p180, p206)

ANDERM/GETTY IMAGES ©

BUDGET
ICELAND

As one of the most expensive countries on the planet, Iceland and affordable in the same sentence may seem like an oxymoron. But there are ways to keep costs down without sacrificing your trip. Shrink car-rental costs, for example, by using public transport, staying in one location, or cycling.

→ MEAL PLANNING

To save, pick up a cool box to store your snacks and picnic lunches on the road. Plan your meals out to a few select recommended spots.

▶ For our top picnic spots, see p72, p151 and p207

Best Affordable Experiences

▶ **Explore Reykjavík on foot and discover some of its unique and quirky sites.** (p76)

▶ **Rent a bike and pedal your way around Reykjavík.** (p50)

▶ **Escape the city, heading east to explore Skaftafell and Vatnajökull National Park.** (p134)

▶ **Unwind in the free Guðlaug geothermal pool at the beach in Akranes.** (p233)

★ BATHING HEAVEN

A quintessential Iceland experience is soaking in the hot tubs of a geothermally heated swimming pool. Admission is cheap and pools are located across the country.

▶ Discover some of the best on p107

Above left Cyclist, Reykjavík
Left Baked goods on display, Reykjavík

ICELAND BEST EXPERIENCES

LET IT
SNOW

▬▬ Long and dark winters don't mean locals stay indoors for half the year. Stay active with outdoor activities year-round and make the most of the snow when it shows. There are ski resorts and backcountry skiing options across the country. For non-skiers, try sledding, snowshoeing or snowmobiling.

Left Snowmobiling, Vatnajökull ice cap **Right** Sailboat cruising, Hornstrandir Nature Reserve **Below** Cross-country skiing near Ólafsfjörður

→ HIT THE SLOPES

Explore near-uncharted territory on a multi-day ski-to-sailboat expedition from Ísafjörður.

▶ Find out more on p212

← ADRENALINE FIX

Race across the wintery landscapes on a snowmobiling tour.

▶ Discover where on p95

↑ SNOW TIME

Cross-country skiing really took off during the Covid-19 pandemic. Book a course in Ólafsfjörður or Siglufjörður.

▶ Learn about skiing and snow play in Akureyri and surrounds on p162

Best Snow Experiences

▶ **Sled across the hills surrounding Akureyri.** (p162)

▶ **Journey to remote backcountry skiing locations in the Westfjords and North Iceland.** (p212, p162)

▶ **Warm up in the hot tub as snowflakes fall from the sky.** (p207)

▶ **Ski under the Northern Lights in Akureyri.** (p162)

▶ **Enjoy winter sport festivals in North Iceland.** (p163)

THE GREAT
OUTDOORS

Pristine nature is really what Iceland is all about. Traverse mountain slopes and wade highland rivers, or ride an Icelandic horse along wild coastlines or past lava landscapes. Once you're done, choose between countless other activities, including kayaking, sailing, skiing, glacier climbing and much, much more.

→ WAY TO THE WATERFALL

Iceland has countless waterfalls. Some, like Glymur (p231), can only be reached on foot – the ultimate reward on your hike.

▶ For more waterfalls, see p92 and p120

Left Landscape along the Laugavegur trail **Right** Glymur **Below** Camper at Skógar

TRAVEL SAFETY & CODE

To stay out of trouble, before setting off on your outdoor adventure, even if it's just a short hike, make sure you've done your research, checked the forecast and have the right gear. And remember to leave the area as you found it – or better still do some plogging along the way!

↑ PITCH YOUR TENT

Experience sleeping outdoors in the midnight sun at some of the country's beautifully situated campgrounds. Þórsmörk in the southern highlands is a local favourite and also has great hikes. If considering camping offsite, first look up 'where you can camp' on ust.is for the latest laws.

▶ Read about hiking in Þórsmörk on p125

Best Outdoor Experiences

▶ Trek the 54km Laugavegur trail between Landmannalaugar and Þórsmörk for a snapshot of Iceland's diverse terrain. (p124)

▶ Take a trip to West Iceland for its myriad hiking trails, like the trail to Glymur waterfall. (p230)

▶ Explore the countryside on horseback. (p192)

▶ Sail to Hornstrandir for a hike in wilderness. (p210)

▶ Lace up your boots and head to BorgarfjörðurEystri for more sublime hiking. (p152)

WATER
WORLD

▬▬▬ Staggering glaciers carved with deep crevasses and hidden ice caves. Coastal fjords rising above colourful fishing villages. Highland rivers journeying to the great blue sea. Iceland is blessed with rich water resources essential for life on the island but also providing a natural playground full of opportunities for discovery.

→ BOUNTY OF THE SEA

Learn about how the ocean sustains life in the Westfjords community of Suðureyri on the Seafood Trail guided walk.

▶ Read more about coastal communities on p204

Left Whale diving near Húsavík **Right** Fishing boats, Suðureyri **Below** Vök Baths

WEIGHTLESS WELLNESS

Many of the country's geothermal pools offer regular relaxation floating sessions using Flothetta, a specially designed floating cap and support for use in water therapy. @samflotfyriralla @flothetta

↑ DON'T MISS

Relax in Vök Baths floating pools on East Iceland's lake Urriðavatn – and take a dip in the chilly lake.

▶ Learn about the Vök Baths on p145

Best Marine Experiences

▶ Sail out to sea in search of the giants of the deep and visit the local whale museum in Húsavík. (p182)

▶ Venture to remote northern islands where small communities live year-round. (p190)

▶ Kick your adrenaline into action on a river rafting trip. (p94)

▶ Get a glimpse of the deep with some cold-water diving. (p167, p202)

▶ Try kayak fishing or birdwatching on water off Snæfellsnes. (p224)

↓ Hafnarfjörður Viking Festival

The peace is shattered as Viking hordes invade Hafnarfjörður for a three-day festival in mid-June. Expect staged fights, storytelling, archery and music.

← National Day

Celebrated on 17 June, Iceland's National Day marks the foundation of the Republic and the country's gaining of independence from Denmark in 1944. Parades, live music, street theatre and more around the country.

For events in Reykjavík, check out 17juni.is.

← Summer Solstice

The midnight sun peaks around 21 June, the longest day of the year, when the sky never goes completely dark. Best enjoyed with an evening hike.

JUNE

Average daytime max: 13°C
Days of rainfall: 9.3 (Reykjavík)

JULY

Iceland in
SUMMER

The summer-festival calendar peaks. Most highland mountain roads are usually open to 4WDs in mid- to late June – sometimes as late as July – and the prime hiking season begins.

↘ Summer Festivals

Reykjavík Pride and Culture Night are highlights of the summer festival calendar.

📍 Reykjavík

▶ p66, p247

↓ Þjóðhátíð

This four-day outdoor festival involves music, dancing, fireworks, a big bonfire, alcohol and a light display with an eruption of red torches – a nod to the island's volcanoes.

📍 Heimaey

▶ p114

Demand for accommodation peaks during summer. Book tours and overnight adventures in advance at lonelyplanet.com/iceland/activities.

AUGUST

ICELAND PLAN BY SEASON

Average daytime max: 14.9°C
Days of rainfall: 10.3

Average daytime max: 14.1°C
Days of rainfall: 11.6

← Berry Picking

Pick wild blueberries, bilberries and crowberries in late August. Try Heiðmörk conservation area.

📍 Heiðmörk

▶ p80

🧳 Packing Notes

Blackout curtains are common, but to block out the bright summer nights pack an eye mask too.

Check out a full calendar of events

The days are still long, but the Northern Lights start to become visible. Some services and attractions are closed; highland roads close in October.

↓ Imagine Peace Tower

Yoko Ono's artwork lights up the sky each year from 9 October, John Lennon's birthday.

📍Viðey Island

▸ imaginepeacetower.com

← Annual Sheep & Horse Round-Ups

Farmers, family and friends come together to round up the sheep from summer pastures in the mountains and valleys. Festive atmosphere. Visitors welcome. The annual horse round-up also takes place.

SEPTEMBER

Average daytime max: 11.4°C
Days of rainfall: 15 (Reykjavík)

OCTOBER

Iceland in
AUTUMN

↓ Iceland Airwaves Music Festival

Reykjavík comes alive with music performances by local and international acts – both emerging and established – in venues across the city.

▶ icelandairwaves.is

↖ Northern Lights

Try to catch a glimpse of the celestial kaleidoscope. Take a tour, or book a few nights at a rural inn and wait for the light show in the evening. Good luck!

Smaller crowds but cooler temperatures. Changing foliage in September and October.

Average daytime max: 7.6°C
Days of rainfall: 13.1

NOVEMBER

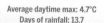

Average daytime max: 4.7°C
Days of rainfall: 13.7

🧳 Packing Notes

A tripod, gloves (fingerless more convenient) and a thermos for nights spent Northern Lights hunting.

← Winter Solstice

The shortest day of the year is around 21 December with four hours of daylight in Reykjavík, less the further north you go.

→ New Year's Eve

The bonfires and fireworks in Reykjavík have become a visitor attraction. Good viewpoints are in front of Perlan and Hallgrímskirkja church.

DECEMBER

Average daytime max: 3.3°C
Days of rainfall: 14.6 (Reykjavík)

JANUARY

Iceland in
WINTER

← New Year's Day Sea Swim

Swimmers descend on Nauthólsvík beach. Inexperienced cold-water swimmers should only spend a few seconds in the water due to the real risk of hypothermia.

● Reykjavík

▶ nautholsvik.is

Best time to see the Northern Lights. Ice caves are accessible. Ski resorts nationwide are usually open from winter to spring.

↓ List í ljósi

A celebration of light returning after the long winter, this festival sees Seyðisfjörður illuminated with art, installations and projections from local and international artists.

← Midwinter Feast

Þorrablót is an old festival in January and February. A buffet of traditional Icelandic food is washed down with Brennivín, Icelandic schnapps. Many restaurants offer a Þorrablót menu.

Average daytime max: 3.2°C
Days of rainfall: 15.3

FEBRUARY

Average daytime max: 3.3°C
Days of rainfall: 15

← Ice Caves

It's safe to access most natural ice caves only from November to March when cool temperatures mean they stop melting. Visit only with a certified tour operator.

 Packing Notes

Bring warm clothes. Also sunglasses – snow and the low winter sun can be blinding, especially when driving.

↓ DesignMarch

Covering all forms of design from fashion to architecture, Iceland's largest design festival brings together local and international exhibitors in the capital.

♥ Reykjavík

▶ designmarch.is

← Aldrei fór ég suður

Held during the Easter long weekend this music festival is a local favourite.

♥ Ísafjörður, the Westfjords

▶ aldrei.is

→ AK Extreme

Held on Hliðarfjall and in downtown Akureyri, North Iceland, this snowboarding and music festival peaks with the big jump contest.

▶ akx.is

MARCH

Average daytime max: 4.2°C
Days of rainfall: 14.2 (Reykjavik)

APRIL

Iceland in
SPRING

↓ Road-Tripping

Improving weather and fewer crowds and lower prices than summer. Road conditions make it a good time to travel the South Coast or the Ring Rd.

↖ First Day of Summer

A public holiday celebrated on the first Thursday after 18 April. Family entertainment held across the country.

MAY

Average daytime max: 6.9°C
Days of rainfall: 12

Average daytime max: 10.1°C
Days of rainfall: 10.8

 Packing Notes

Layered clothing is key in changeable spring weather. Don't forget a waterproof and breathable outer layer.

0 — 1 km
0 — 0.5 miles

REYKJAVÍK
Trip Builder

**TAKE YOUR PICK OF MUST-SEES
AND HIDDEN GEMS**

▬▬▬▬ From a grim, seemingly
endless night in winter to
incomprehensibly bright nights
in summer. A chill and laid-back
mood during daytime to a dynamic
nightlife. Reykjavík is a big city in a
tiny package next door to nature.

🗺 Trip Notes

Hub town Reykjavík

How long Allow 1 week, including day trips
away from the capital

Getting around Many places can be
visited on foot or with rental scooters and
bikes. Bus transit is decent, but car rental
may be a good choice too.

Tips Depending on your style of travel,
renting a car and exploring on your own
may be a cheaper option than going on
guided tours.

Grótta
Stroll on the beach at
the tip of the Reykjavík
peninsula. Find the small
warm pool. If you're lucky,
you can even walk out to
the lighthouse.
🕐 *1hr walk from Grandi*

Old Downtown & Laugavegur
Uncover the history of Reykjavík
among the pubs and cafes; see
the countless cats of the capital
and have a taste of Iceland.
🕐 *1hr walk from Grótta*

Öskjuhlíð
Woodlands close to the city
centre. Explore the WWII
bunkers, encounter curious
rabbits and perhaps end by
taking a swim in the sea in
Nauthólsvík geothermal beach.
🕐 *40min walk from Downtown*

Akure

SELTJARNARNES

Eiðsgran

ICELAND BUILD YOUR TRIP

Grandi

Discover the hidden diamonds in the old fishing district of Reykjavík. Grandi is home to many cultural and culinary gems.

🕐 *20min walk from Downtown*

Viðey

Board the ferry to iconic Viðey and explore a diverse collection of outdoor art, witness the massive avian fauna of the island and enjoy the proximity to the sea.

🕐 *5min ferry from Skarfabakki*

Viðey

Engey

Skarfabakki Harbour

Sundahöfn Harbour

GRANDI/ ÖRFIRISEY

Old Harbour

Hringbraut

OLD REYKJAVÍK

Sæbraut

Hverfisgata

Sæbraut

Borgartún

Sundlaugavegur

Elliðaárdalur & Around

Take a long walk, cool your feet in the river or simply enjoy the outdoors while picnicking. Visit Árbæjarsafn outdoor museum for a twisted doughnut.

🕐 *15min drive from Downtown*

Tjörnin

LAUGAVEGUR

LAUGARDALUR

MELAR

Suðurgata

Gamla

Hringbraut

Snorrabraut

Raudarárstígur

TÚN

Laugavegur

Sigtún

Laugavegur

Laugardalur

Kringlumýrarbraut

VATNSMÝRI

Búsðavegur

Langahlíð

HÁALEITI NORTH

Háaleitisbraut

Suðurlandsbraut

Einarsnes

Miklabraut

SLEIFAN

Nauthólsvík Geothermal Beach

HÁALEITI SOUTH

Háaleitisbraut

Miklabraut

Sogavegur

GERÐI

Hæðargarður

Vesturlandsvegur

Reykjanesbraut

Elliðaá

Elliðaárdalur

Hafnarfjörður Old Town

Overlook Hafnarfjörður from Hamarinn cliff, walk through the old town, visit Hafnarborg Museum and have coffee at Pallett. Maybe you'll see hidden people?

🕐 *25min drive from Downtown*

Heiðmörk

Visit Heiðmörk at the edge of the city, a seemingly endless source of outdooring that shows that Reykjavík is, in fact, next door to nature.

🕐 *35min drive from Downtown*

Heiðmörk (12km)

Hafnarfjörður (9km); Keflavík International Airport (45km)

THE RING ROAD
Trip Builder

TAKE YOUR PICK OF MUST-SEES AND HIDDEN GEMS

▬▬▬ Eyes on the road. This famous 1332km loop connects most towns and villages via mountain passes, one-lane bridges and diverse scenery. Many of Iceland's most iconic sites are literally roadside, as if the road were designed as an excursion.

🗺 Trip Notes

Hub towns Selfoss, Höfn, Egilsstaðir, Akureyri, Borgarnes

How long Allow 7 days

Getting around For the ultimate road trip, hire a car. Otherwise, buses run year-round, but have a sporadic schedule outside summer.

Tips Monitor weather forecasts and road conditions, particularly for the mountain passes on Holtavörðuheiði and Öxnadalsheiði. If you don't have driving experience in snow and ice, consider joining a tour. Summer traffic is heavy between Selfoss and Vík. And watch out for sheep!

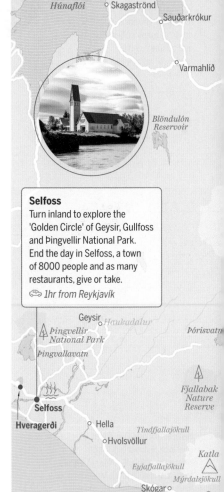

Siglufjörður •

Skagafjörður

Drangey

Húnaflói ○ Skagaströnd

○ Sauðarkrókur

○ Varmahlíð

Blöndulón Reservoir

Selfoss
Turn inland to explore the 'Golden Circle' of Geysir, Gullfoss and Þingvellir National Park. End the day in Selfoss, a town of 8000 people and as many restaurants, give or take.
🚗 *1hr from Reykjavík*

Geysir ○ *Haukadalur*

🏕 *Þingvellir National Park*   *Þórisvatn*

Þingvallavatn

🏕 *Fjallabak Nature Reserve*

♨ **Selfoss**

Hveragerði ○ Hella

○ Hvolsvöllur *Tindfjallajökull*

Katla 🔺

Eyjafjallajökull 🔺 *Mýrdalsjökull*

Skógar ○

Vestmannaeyjar Islands ○ Vestmannaeyjar

Vík

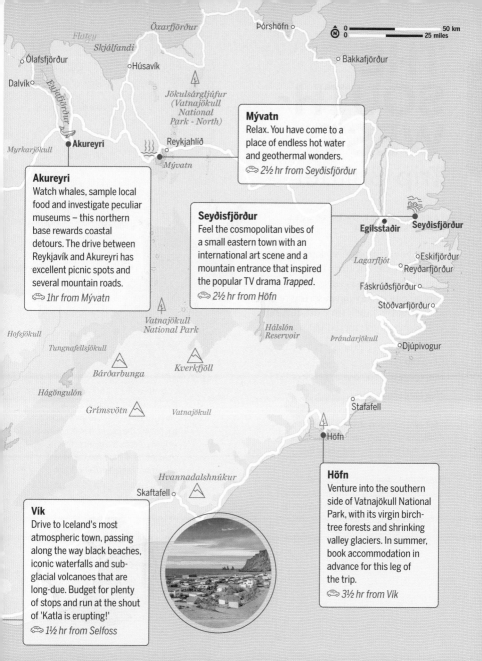

Mývatn
Relax. You have come to a place of endless hot water and geothermal wonders.
🚗 2½ hr from Seyðisfjörður

Akureyri
Watch whales, sample local food and investigate peculiar museums – this northern base rewards coastal detours. The drive between Reykjavík and Akureyri has excellent picnic spots and several mountain roads.
🚗 1hr from Mývatn

Seyðisfjörður
Feel the cosmopolitan vibes of a small eastern town with an international art scene and a mountain entrance that inspired the popular TV drama *Trapped*.
🚗 2½ hr from Höfn

Höfn
Venture into the southern side of Vatnajökull National Park, with its virgin birch-tree forests and shrinking valley glaciers. In summer, book accommodation in advance for this leg of the trip.
🚗 3½ hr from Vík

Vík
Drive to Iceland's most atmospheric town, passing along the way black beaches, iconic waterfalls and sub-glacial volcanoes that are long-due. Budget for plenty of stops and run at the shout of 'Katla is erupting!'
🚗 1½ hr from Selfoss

Öxarfjörður
Þórshöfn
0 — 50 km
0 — 25 miles
Flatey
Skjálfandi
Bakkafjörður
Ólafsfjörður
Húsavík
Dalvík
Jökulsárgljúfur (Vatnajökull National Park - North)
Myrkárjökull
Akureyri
Reykjahlíð
Mývatn
Egilsstaðir
Seyðisfjörður
Eskifjörður
Lagarfljót
Reyðarfjörður
Fáskrúðsfjörður
Stöðvarfjörður
Vatnajökull National Park
Hofsjökull
Hálslón Reservoir
Þrándarjökull
Djúpivogur
Tungnafellsjökull
Bárðarbunga
Kverkfjöll
Hágöngulón
Grímsvötn
Vatnajökull
Stafafell
Höfn
Hvannadalshnúkur
Skaftafell

THE SOUTH-WEST
Trip Builder

TAKE YOUR PICK OF MUST-SEES AND HIDDEN GEMS

■■■ For adventure seekers who want big bang for their bucks. The Southwest region is close to the capital city of Reykjavík so you're not spending too much time driving, but still seeing some incredible sights.

🗺 Trip Notes

Hub towns Keflavík, Reykjavík, Selfoss, Vík

How long Allow 1 week

Getting around Rent a car to drive at your own pace and stop at hidden gems. Alternatively, if you want to sit back and enjoy the view, join an organised tour group.

Tips June to August is peak tourist season. Be prepared for the crowds. Roads are paved and well maintained but can be difficult in winter conditions.

30 km
15 miles

Borgarnes

Borgarfjörður

Akranes

Faxaflói Reykjavík

Kópavogur

Miðnes Hafnarfjörður

Keflavík *Reykjanesfólkvangur Wilderness Reserve*

Reykjanes Peninsula Fagradalsfjall

Seltún

Grindavíko

Reykjanestá

Reykjanes Peninsula
This usually overlooked area packs a big punch: the jagged basalt columns of Reykjanestá, the geothermal mudpots of Seltún, and the newest attraction: Fagradalsfjall volcano.
🚗 *1hr from Reykjavík to Reykjanestá*

The Golden Circle

Walk between continents at þingvellir, watch bubbling geysers spout into the air at Haukadalur valley and take in the thunderous roar of Gullfoss waterfall.

🚗 *2hr from Reykjanestá to Haukadalur*

Landmannalaugar

Multicoloured mountains, lava fields, geothermal hot springs and unlimited hiking. Note: only accessible via 4WD or bus from June to September.

🚗 *3¼ hr from þórsmörk*

Þingvellir National Park

Haukadalur
Geysir ○ *Gulfoss*

Golden Circle

Þingvallavatn

Fjallabak Nature Reserve

þórsmörk

A hikers' paradise of lush green mountains and glaciers in the rugged highlands. Between June and September, drive a 4WD or hop on a bus, or take a guided super-Jeep tour year-round.

🚗 *1½ hr from Vík*

● **Hveragerði**

Ölfusa ● **Selfoss**

Þorlákshöfn ○ *Flóahreppur*

Hella ○

Tindfjallajökull

○ Hvolsvöllur

South Coast

Known for massive waterfalls, breathtaking glaciers and black-sand beaches, the South Coast hosts some of the country's most iconic landmarks.

🚗 *1hr from Haukadalur to Selfoss*

Mýrdalsjökull

Eyjafjallajökull

△ *Katla*

Sólheimajökull

○ Skógar

Heimaey ○

Vestmannaeyjar Islands

Vík

Vík

A charming coastal village and a great place to stay the night after all your South Coast adventures.

🚗 *1½ hr from Selfoss*

THE NORTH
Trip Builder

TAKE YOUR PICK OF MUST-SEES AND HIDDEN GEMS

▬▬▬ Experience the North by boat or horse, discover varied waterfalls and geothermal gems, hike birding trails or snow-covered summits and ski to the shore. Also remember to take it easy, explore the cultural scene and go for a swim.

🗺 Trip Notes

Hub towns Hvammstangi, Blönduós, Akureyri, Húsavík

How long Allow 10 days

Getting around Best to hire a car. You can also travel by bus, SBA highland bus or plane between the South and North.

Tips Highland roads are open in summer and require a highland-suited 4WD. ICE-SAR patrols the region and assists with river crossings (the driver is always responsible). See safetravel.is for more information.

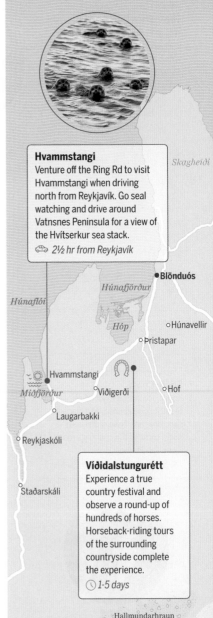

Hvammstangi
Venture off the Ring Rd to visit Hvammstangi when driving north from Reykjavík. Go seal watching and drive around Vatnsnes Peninsula for a view of the Hvítserkur sea stack.
🚗 2½ hr from Reykjavík

Skagheiði

●Blönduós

Húnafjörður

Húnaflói

Hóp   ○Húnavellir

○Þristapar

☼≈ Hvammstangi   ⌒
Miðfjörður   ○Viðigerði   ○Hof

○Laugarbakki

○Reykjaskóli

○Staðarskáli

Víðidalstungurétt
Experience a true country festival and observe a round-up of hundreds of horses. Horseback-riding tours of the surrounding countryside complete the experience.
🕐 1-5 days

Hallmundarhraun

Skagafjörður

Siglufjörður

Skjálfandi

Tjörnes

Ólafsfjörður

Húsavík

Fell

Málmey

Tröllaskagi
Peninsula

Dalvík

Grenivík

Laxamýri

Hofsós

The Diamond Circle
This 250km tourist route in Northeast Iceland includes the region's best-known attractions: waterfalls, volcanoes, whale watching and geothermal baths.
🚗 3½ hr from Hrafnagil to Húsavík

Viðvík

Eyjafjörður

Laufás

Sauðárkrókur

Tröllaskagi
This peninsula between Skagafjörður and Eyjafjörður is characterised by tall, rugged mountains and small glaciers, great for hiking and skiing of all adventure levels.
🚗 2hr from Akureyri to Hofsós

Akureyri

Hofstaðir

Reynisstaður

Eyjafjarðarsveit
A centre for dairy production and other agriculture. Discover quirky museums, countryside churches and local food, and enjoy quiet contemplation in nature.
🚗 15min from Akureyri to Hrafnagil

Hrafnagil

Varmahlíð

Bólstaðarhlíð

Blöndulón
Reservoir

Hveravellir
Road F35 lies across the ancient highland route of Kjölur between Langjökull and Hofsjökull glaciers. A 4WD is required. Stay to explore the highlands from Hveravellir.
🚗 2½ hr from Hvammstangi

 Hveravellir

Langjökull

Vatnajökull
National
Park

THE WEST
Trip Builder

TAKE YOUR PICK OF MUST-SEES AND HIDDEN GEMS

▬▬▬ Go west to discover the road less travelled and explore a bounty of fjords, hot springs, islands, glaciers, mountains, waterfalls and stunning coastlines. The region also boasts culinary and cultural highlights.

🗺 Trip Notes

Hub towns Borgarnes, Stykkishólmur, Patreksfjörður, Ísafjörður

How long Allow 2 weeks

Getting around Hire a car and travel at your own pace. Organised tours are also available. Buses run to some destinations but are infrequent.

Tips Most roads are sealed, but allow extra time for slow and safe driving on gravel roads in the Westfjords and when roads are icy. Some services have limited opening hours, are by appointment only, or are closed October through April.

0 — 40 km
0 — 20 miles

Suðureyri ○

Þingeyri
Enjoy coffee and Belgian waffles at cosy Simbahöllin cafe. Play golf, hire a mountain bike, join a horse-riding tour or climb nearby Sandafell or Kaldbakur mountains.
🚗 2hr from Patreksfjörður

Þingeyri ●

Bíldudalur ○

Patreksfjörður ●
⚓

Brekkuvellir ○

Patreksfjörður
Base yourself in this small fishing village for a trip to Látrabjarg bird cliffs and golden-red Rauðasandur beach. Grab a meal at Flak arts venue, pub and restaurant.
🚗 2¼ hr from Breiðafjörður, including ferry

Hellissandur ○   Grundarfjörður ○
● Ólafsvík

Snæfellsjökull National Park △

Snæfellsnes
Explore the region's national park and journey to the top of Snæfellsjökull glacier. Kayak near iconic Kirkjufell mountain, go whale and wildlife watching and dine in colourful Stykkishólmur.
🚗 1¼ hr from Borgarnes to Stykkishólmur

Búrfell

Hornstrandir
Nature Reserve

Bolungarvík

Drangajökull

Ísafjörður

Suðavík

Lóndjúp

Ísafjörður

Join your adventure tours of choice, from kayaking, hiking, diving, cycling and wildlife watching to sailing and snow sports. Visit Hornstrandir Nature Reserve and nearby villages such as Suðureyri.

🚗 *45min from Þingeyri*

Vatnsfjörður
Nature Reserve

Hólmavík

Húnaflói

Hólmavík

Inform yourself at the Sheep Farming Museum (11km from town) or Museum of Sorcery and Witchcraft. Soak up warm water and views at nearby Drangses Hot Tubs.

🚗 *2½ hr from Ísafjörður*

Breiðafjörður

Take the ferry from Stykkishólmur to Flatey island to disconnect, get close to nature and savour local ingredients at the hotel restaurant.

⛴ *1½ hr from Stykkishólmur*

Breiðafjörður

Hvammstangi

Reykjaskóli

Stykkishólmur

Akranes

Make this harbour town the start or end of your journey. Hike nearby Akrafjall and take a dip in Guðlaug Baths on Langisandur beach, popular with sea swimmers.

🚗 *45min from Reykjavík*

Birfröst

Borgarfjörður

Discover a fjord full of surprises. Learn about the sagas at the Settlement Centre, take in Hraunfossar and Barnafoss waterfalls, explore Langjökull ice tunnel and relax in the Húsafell Canyon Baths.

🚗 *30min from Akranes to Borgarnes*

● **Borgarnes**

Akranes ⚓

Hvalfjörður

7 Things to Know About
ICELAND

INSIDER TIPS TO HIT THE GROUND RUNNING

1 Fragile Environment

Iceland is a nature lover's paradise, but its vegetation is delicate due to the harsh climate and short growing season. Moss can take years to recover after being damaged by footprints or tyre marks. Going off the beaten track and removing rocks to make cairns can also cause erosion. Off-road driving can cause irreparable damage and is punishable by huge fines.

▶ Get more tips on how to leave a lighter footprint on p242

2 Geothermal Energy

Hot springs, volcanic fumaroles, mudpots and that sulphurous 'rotten egg' smell from hot-water taps are signs of geothermal energy. Hydropower is the main source of electricity, but geothermal makes up most of the rest. The hot water is used to heat buildings, greenhouses, swimming pools and keep footpaths ice-free in winter.

▶ Learn more about volcanoes on p110

3 Ring Road

A road trip along Iceland's national highway gives you a taste of the best the country has to offer. Watch out for one-lane bridges and animals on the road and don't try to see it all in a weekend.

▶ Discover the Ring Road on p16

4 Alphabet

The Icelandic alphabet has 32 letters. You might not be familiar with these ones:

Ð ð – as 'th' in 'rather'

Þ þ – as 'th' in 'thin'

Æ æ – as 'ai' in 'aisle'

Ö ö – as 'u' in 'nurse'

▶ Learn more about the Icelandic language on p248

6 Pools & Etiquette

All that geothermal energy means nearly every town has a swimming pool. Most poolgoers don't actually swim, but a soak in the hot tub is a daily ritual for many. There's usually a steam bath; some have a sauna and, more recently, a cold tub too. Entry is cheap.

To uphold hygiene and lower chlorine levels, visitors must thoroughly shower with soap without a swimsuit before entering. There are separate change rooms for men and women – and gender-neutral areas at some. Some pools have a private shower, but mostly showers are communal. Having grown up with this, Icelanders don't bat an eyelid when they run into each other naked.

Trying to get out of the mandatory no-swimsuit shower will only draw attention. It's frowned upon so don't be surprised if the person standing next to you or the shower warden points out the rules. Just dive in.

▶ Prepare yourself with the dos and don'ts of pool etiquette on p104

5 Northern Lights

The aurora borealis are only visible when it's dark – so not in summer – and the less cloud cover the better. They are often even visible in downtown Reykjavík, but less light pollution is best, so head away from built-up areas to really see the sky come alive.

▶ For the best spots to see the Northern Lights, see p174

7 Wild Weather

Icelandic weather is notoriously fickle. Don't be surprised if it's rainy and cold in summer – or you get all four seasons in one. But you didn't come to Iceland for warm and sunny weather. Be prepared, wear layers and embrace it! The landscape is still stunning.

▶ Discover the best – and worst – of Iceland's seasons on p24

Read, Listen, Watch & Follow

 READ

Independent People (Halldór Laxness; 1934–35) Classic novel filled with satire and humour by the 1955 Nobel laureate.

The Little Books Series (Alda Sigmundsdóttir; 2012–) Series providing insight into Iceland's culture and people.

The Blue Fox (Sjón; 2013) Award-winning mystery set in winter 1883.

How Iceland Changed the World: The Big History of a Small Island (Egill Bjarnason; 2021) Iceland's role in historical events.

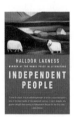

 LISTEN

Medúlla (Björk; 2004) Almost entirely an a cappella album. Recorded with choirs, a throat singer and a beatboxer.

Kveðja (Bríet; 2020) Icelandic-language pop- and country-influenced release. Icelandic Music Awards Album of the Year.

Arabian Horse (GusGus; 2011) Dance pop and eighth studio album by the Reykjavík electro outfit.

Sól rís 1980-2020 (Bubbi Morthens; 2020) Bubbi is a local legend whose career has spanned punk, rock, blues, reggae and folk.

MELANIE LEMAHIEU/SHUTTERSTOCK ©

Haglél (Mugison; 2011) Blues-rock and first Icelandic-language album by this Westfjords local. Another Icelandic Music Awards Album of the Year.

▷ WATCH

101 Reykjavík (2000) Award-winning dark comedy and director Baltasar Kormákur's first feature film.

Angels of the Universe (2000) Tragic comedy dealing in part with mental illness and reactions to it.

Jar City (2006) Crime thriller based on Arnaldur Indriðason's best-selling novel.

I Remember You (2017) Mystery horror film about people who move to an abandoned town.

Trapped TV Series (2015–) Crime drama series by Baltasar Kormákur set in remote Iceland.

TOP: AF ARCHIVE/ALAMY STOCK PHOTO © BLUEEYES PRODUCTIONS
BOTTOM: TCD/PROD.DB/ALAMY STOCK PHOTO ©

▲ FOLLOW

The Reykjavík Grapevine
(@rvkgrapevine)
News, life, culture and travel magazine and website.

 All Things Iceland
(@allthingsiceland)
Expat view of life in Iceland.

 Benjamin Hardman
(@benjaminhardman)
Photographer and filmmaker.

 Gunnar Freyr Gunnarsson
(@icelandic_explorer)
Reykjavík-based photographer and storyteller.

ˈÁSˌ
Ása Steinarsdóttir
(@asasteinars)
Photographer and adventure content.

 ↘ **Get in the mood with the perfect playlist at lonelyplanet.com/articles/playlist-for-iceland-road-trip**

REYKJAVÍK

FOOD | CULTURE | MUSIC

Experience
Reykjavík
online

Bonus Online Experiences

▶ **Reykjavík with Kids**

▶ **The Whale Fjord & Waterfalls**

Roam the beach and find the footbath at **Grótta** (p80)
🕐 *1 day*

Discover cultural and culinary gems in **Grandi** fishing district (p55)
🕐 *1 day*

S E L T J A R N A R N E S

Stroll through the various **Reykjavík Art Museum** locations (p71)
🕐 *1 day*

Unearth how people lived at the **Settlement Exhibiton** (p77)
🕐 *½ day*

Akurey

G R A N D I *Old Harbour*

Mýrargata

O L D
R E Y K J A V Í K

Hringbraut

Tjörnin

Suðurgata

Hringbraut

REYKJAVÍK
Trip Builder

▬▬▬ Care to take a bath by the seaside? Would you like to meet farm animals in the city? Or do you want to prowl for food and drinks in the darkest days of winter? Reykjavík offers plenty no matter the season.

Explore Icelandic history at the **National Museum of Iceland** (p72)
🕐 *½ day*

Explore bookable experiences in Reykjavík online

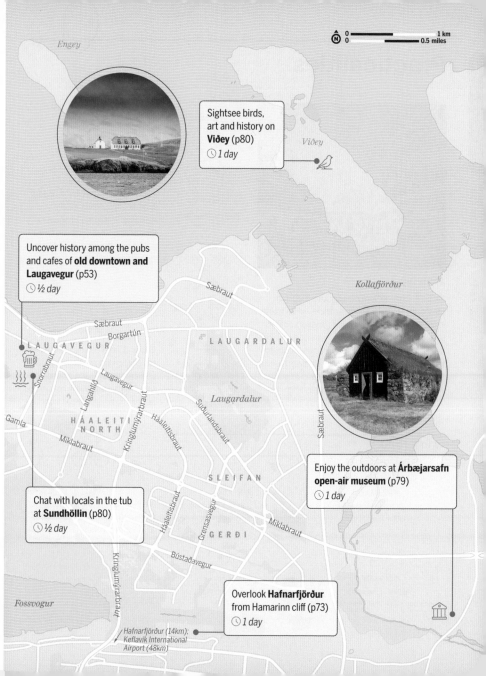

Sightsee birds, art and history on **Viðey** (p80)
🕐 1 day

Uncover history among the pubs and cafes of **old downtown and Laugavegur** (p53)
🕐 ½ day

Chat with locals in the tub at **Sundhöllin** (p80)
🕐 ½ day

Enjoy the outdoors at **Árbæjarsafn open-air museum** (p79)
🕐 1 day

Overlook **Hafnarfjörður** from Hamarinn cliff (p73)
🕐 1 day

Engey

Viðey

Kollafjörður

Sæbraut

Sæbraut

Borgartún

LAUGAVEGUR

Snorrabraut

Laugavegur

Langahlíð

Kringlumýrarbraut

Háaleitisbraut

Suðurlandsbraut

LAUGARDALUR

Laugardalur

Sæbraut

Gamla

HÁALEITI NORTH

Miklabraut

SLEIFAN

Háaleitisbraut

Grensásvegur

GERÐI

Miklabraut

Bústaðavegur

Kringlumýrarbraut

Fossvogur

Hafnarfjörður (14km);
Keflavík International
Airport (48km)

0   1 km
0   0.5 miles
N

Practicalities

ARRIVING

Keflavík Internationl Airport About 40 minutes' drive from Reykjavík. As there are no trains in Iceland, there are two main transport options to and from the airport: the flybus and a taxi. The flybus makes stops in a few places on its way to the BSÍ terminal, right next to downtown. From there taxis are usually the best option to reach your destination, although walking is also viable.

HOW MUCH FOR A

Happy-hour beer 900kr

Icelandic hot dog 600kr

Bus fare 490kr

GETTING AROUND

Walking While the capital region is quite large, it's definitely walkable. Within a 30-minute radius of downtown, you can find a public beach, museums, galleries, restaurants and more.

Bus and Taxi For longer distances, the city bus is a relatively rapid and convenient way to get around. Try the Strætó.is app. While not cheap, taxis are just a phone call away.

Cycling Rental scooters and bikes are plentiful around town and can be rented via various apps such as Hopp and Wind. They're a swift and delightful way to explore Reykjavík.

WHEN TO GO

MAR–MAY
Expect wind and rain; great for a cultural visit in the city.

JUN–AUG
The ideal season for excursions and outdoor activities.

SEP–NOV
A relatively calm season; outdoors and cultural activities.

DEC–FEB
Ideal for winter sports and cultural activities.

EATING & DRINKING

Laugavegur The main shopping street in Iceland, Laugavegur and its surroundings hold a huge variety of restaurants and pubs.

Grandi The Old Harbour is home to a diverse collection of cultural and culinary spots. (pictured; p55)

Must-try craft-beer pub Brewdog has a really good menu of Icelandic breweries on tap at all times and knowledgeable staff. (p78)

Best food court Hlemmur Mathöll is a small but characteristic food court in a famous bus terminal in Reykjavík. Once home to many questionable characters it is mainly populated by hungry and outgoing locals and travellers alike. (pictured; p54)

CONNECT & FIND YOUR WAY

Wi-Fi and mobile networks Available for use everywhere you go. Wi-fi access codes are displayed openly in most cafes, bars and restaurants. 4G SIM cards are also relatively affordable.

Navigation software This is pretty accurate in Iceland. Furthermore, locals will most often know the way if you ask around.

WHERE TO STAY

Accommodation is expensive in Iceland, but there are feasible midrange options, as well as a wide variety of rentals via Airbnb and similar services.

Neighbourhood	Pro/Con
Downtown	The liveliest part of the capital area. Significantly higher prices, but closer to most things.
Kópavogur & Hafnarfjörður	These two capital-area towns offer cheaper accommodation, but at the cost of 30-minute bus rides to downtown.
Anywhere else in the capital area	Rental apartments available around town; different locations with their own pros and cons.

REYKJAVÍK CITY CARD

The Reykjavík City Card is available online in 24-, 48- and 72-hour variations. Includes access to the bus system and a trip to Viðey, various museums and more.

MONEY

Visa and MasterCard are accepted just about everywhere. Low-cost supermarkets (Bónus and Krónan) are great for stocking up on snacks and groceries.

01

Eat
REYKJAVÍK

RESTAURANTS | PUBS | FOOD

Looking for a place to eat? Strolling through downtown or nearby Grandi (the old fishing harbour) is a worthwhile and enjoyable way of discovering culinary gems. Offerings include 'honest' burgers, New Icelandic cuisine and fish courses. Work up an appetite by sightseeing historical and cultural spots, and much more.

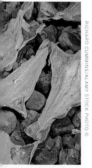

How to

Getting around Most buses go downtown, and from there it's an easy and enjoyable walk out to Grandi (10 minutes). Other options include grabbing a taxi or riding the bus, which has regular stops all through downtown.

Electric scooters or bikes are available for rent via countless app services.

Cost There are both cheap and expensive options in the area. Sit-down dinner easily averages 2500kr to 3000kr per person, excluding drinks.

REYKJAVIK EXPERIENCES

JON PALL VILHELMSSON ©

ICELANDIC PHOTO AGENCY/ALAMY STOCK PHOTO ©

Out on the Town

Iceland's foodie scene has grown exponentially in the past 15 years. New locations of various sizes and price ranges proliferate, as do progressive attempts at exploring Icelandic cuisine, and the number of luxurious or unique food experiences.

A significant portion of restaurants can be found downtown: on Laugavegur, the main shopping street; on Hverfisgata; and in and around Kvosin, the oldest part of the city. Strolling around downtown is both an architectural and gastronomical delight.

Café Loki serves home-style Icelandic dishes. In good weather, sit outside the cafe to enjoy the views of Hallgrímskirkja church and the constant flow of people. **Mat Bar** is an excellent choice for a more intimate dinner

RICHARD CUMMINS/ALAMY STOCK PHOTO ©

🏛 Maritime Museum

The main attraction at this Old Harbour museum is an exhibition called *Fish and People – 150 Years of Maritime History*. It offers an interactive insight into the culinary past and present-day fishing industry, walking you through the phases of seafaring, fishing and production.

Top left Flatus, Kex Hostel **Top right** Herring plate, Café Loki **Left** Dried cod

experience, sharing Nordic–Italian fusion dishes and tasting wine in the tight but lovely restaurant. **Flatus** at Kex Hostel has great pizzas on a budget, not to mention a good selection of Icelandic craft beers.

The **Hlemmur Food Court** downtown has been added to the bus station. The crown jewel of Hlemmur, **Skál!** serves reasonably priced courses of fine-dining quality, alongside a decent selection of wines and Icelandic craft beer. There's something magical about

fine-dining among the buses. **Flatey Pizza** is another great option in Hlemmur, serving very good stone-baked napolitanas from traditional sour fermented dough. Other options include **Fuego Taqueria**, which serves four types of LA-style tacos.

The Old Harbour

It feels natural to dine at the Old Harbour, but to this day there are boats still coming in. It's home to a range of restaurants, cafes and

✖ Reykjavík's Best Bites

Dill The only Michelin-starred restaurant in Iceland (p78).

ÓX A speakeasy-style restaurant (p78).

Mat Bar A stylish spot with a good vibe (p53).

Skál! A top-tier restaurant at the bus station (above).

Coocoos Nest A family-run restaurant at the Old Harbour.

Ólafur Örn Ólafsson
TV personality, owner of Tíu Sopar, Honkytonk BBQ and Brút Restaurant.

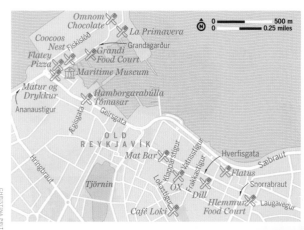

Left Sommelier pours wine at Dill Restaurant **Below** Marshall House, home to La Primavera

bars, mixed in with cultural attractions, ice-cream parlours and light industry.

Among the Old Harbour dining options is **Matur og Drykkur** (p58), which reimagines classical Icelandic dishes, presenting them in a six-course menu. It also has a fantastic wine-pairing menu. **La Primavera** is located in Marshall House (which also houses the Living Art Museum, Kling & Bang gallery, i8 Grandi and the private studio of artist Ólafur Elíasson). It's a perfect chaser after exploring the art. Located in a tiny house on the fringe of the Old Harbour, **Hamborgarabúlla Tómasar** is the burger joint of choice. It serves honest burgers and fries, no hassle and no trying to be anything more than just that.

Grandi Food Court is located in a building that used to serve as a fish factory but was later repurposed into spaces for entrepreneurs, among other things. In good weather you can drink and eat outside while overlooking the harbour and the downtown opposite. In the food court, **Kore** serves Korean fusion street food, including Korean-style tacos and its so-called 'filthy fries'. Also in the food court, **Fjárhúsið** (Sheep House) specialises in Icelandic lamb. It serves excellent lamb variations on hamburgers, fajitas, pitas and sandwiches. Then head over to **Omnom**, offering premium Icelandic bean-to-bar chocolate and ice-cream.

Icelandic
FOOD

01 Blood sausage

Sheep's blood, mixed with lard and grains, is stuffed into animal intestines, sewn shut and boiled. To this day, it's widely available.

02 Lamb

By many considered the pinnacle of Icelandic raw ingredients, lamb is both a tasty and affordable meat. Available in most restaurants.

03 Foal meat

Icelanders love to ride their horses, but perhaps less known is that Icelanders love to eat them too.

04 Rice pudding

Hardly Icelandic cuisine, or is it? Contrary to everywhere else in the world, Icelanders consider rice pudding to be dinner, not breakfast or dessert.

05 Skyr

You've heard of *skyr*, right? The Icelandic yoghurt is, in fact, not a yoghurt but more akin to cheese.

06 Blueberries

One of only a handful of berries that grow wild in Iceland, blueberries are a delicacy that are commonly enjoyed soaked in cream.

07 Fermented shark

More commonly eaten as an appetiser or with a shot of Icelandic Brennivín, fermented shark is not as strong-smelling as the skate.

08 Salted fish

Before coolers, fish was kept consumable by being kept in salt. Salted fish with boiled potatoes is still a common dinner option in Icelandic homes.

09 Fermented skate

A traditional Christmas Eve dish. Also an item of controversy that traditionally causes feuds in apartment buildings because of the rancid smell from the preparation of it.

10 Brennivín

Until 1989 beer was banned in Iceland. Strong alcohol like Brennivín were the go-to drinks for many until then.

11 Coffee

While not necessarily sophisticated in terms of the art of coffee, Icelanders take coffee very seriously and consider it a staple of their identity.

12 Rye bread

Probably the most Icelandic bread you can get. It comes in solid, square pieces that are sometimes even baked in geothermal hot springs.

13 Fish jerky

The true sports snack of Iceland. Lightweight, high in protein and very chewy.

A New Icelandic Cuisine

TEACHING OLD FOOD NEW TRICKS

The first thing that comes to mind when most people think about Icelandic cuisine is probably sheep, fish and a variety of strange courses that unaccustomed diners may find daunting. New Icelandic cuisine puts a modern twist on many of these traditional staples and repays intrepid eaters for their sense of culinary adventure.

Left Kombu with Brennivín sauce **Middle** Matur og Drykkur **Right** Ling with root vegetable mousse, celery root and carrot salad

For most locals, talking about Icelandic cuisine is more akin to talking about old Icelandic food-preservation methods – the conversation can get pretty academic. Generally speaking, travellers may find the look, smell and taste of true Icelandic cuisine challenging. In fact, a quick search on social media will show that people see Icelandic cuisine more as a test of their character and tolerance rather than, well, actual cuisine.

But knowledge, preconceptions and stories colour people's reactions too, and when it comes to Icelandic ingredients, those preconceptions present a great challenge – and, perhaps, a great opportunity.

Uncharted Territory

Ólafur Júlíusson is floor manager at Matur og Drykkur. To meet the challenges that recent years have thrown at the tourism and restaurant industries, Matur og Drykkur reduced its menu to a single culinary experience that would be rotated and rediscovered continuously. According to Ólafur, this metamorphosis has had a huge positive effect: 'We're never turning back.'

Having a single menu has its challenges and its benefits. He admits that sometimes locals wrinkle their noses at courses they generally don't associate with fine dining: blood pudding, cods' heads, bean or cocoa soup. Ólafur concedes that Icelanders may suffer from an inferiority complex based on their gastronomical heritage, before adding: 'But it certainly doesn't have to be that way.'

The restaurant works almost exclusively with locally sourced ingredients and focuses on delivering Icelandic

cuisine in an unfamiliar shape and form. It uses a diverse set of local suppliers, obtaining – among other things – rhubarb and rhubarb juice for cocktails, and goat cheese and meat from places like Háafell farm.

Some ingredients the chefs themselves go out and harvest, such as oarweed, chervil and wild celery. This approach enhances sustainability and results in a barely noticeable carbon footprint without compromising Matur og Drykkur's primary goal: to make great food and present diners with a unique take on Icelandic dishes.

> People see Icelandic cuisine more as a test of their character and tolerance rather than, well, actual cuisine.

Stories Behind the Food

While storytelling isn't the main selling point of Matur og Drykkur, there's a story nonetheless behind each and every course on the menu. These stories include the methods to which early Icelanders resorted to survive winter, the ingredients they had to choose from, and how those dishes coloured their attitude towards food culture. Then there's the story behind each ingredient, from knowing that the goat cheese comes from a farm whose goats got their 15 minutes of fame in *Game of Thrones* to learning that the Atlantic halibut on the menu is yesterday's catch. And as you walk out after a night at Matur og Drykkur, you'll have stories of your own. Travellers intrepid enough to eat cod's head or savour blood pudding in blueberry sauce will never look at Icelandic cuisine the same way.

✂ Fermented Shark

Some of the foods in question have been described as vulgar and disgusting. In the case of the local fermented shark, Anthony Bourdain himself claimed that it was 'the single worst, most disgusting and terrible tasting thing' that he had ever tasted. Gordon Ramsay famously spat it out, and Ainsley Harriott claimed it was 'like chewing a urine-infested mattress'. Archaeologist Neil Oliver, researching Viking diets, claimed it was like 'blue cheese but a hundred times stronger'. Although they laugh it off, deep down Icelanders can't blame them. The locals know what the critics are talking about.

02 Into the
NIGHT

NIGHTLIFE | CLUBS | BARS

You're in a new town and you've been craving a night out for the longest while, but don't know where to start. This handy guide – based on the habits of a resident creature of the night – was written to help you find your way around the Icelandic party scene. Now get out: party like an Icelander.

🗺 How to

Getting around

The Reykjavík club scene is concentrated around downtown, on and around Laugavegur, and in the old downtown.

When to go All year round as long as it's evening. Dress for the weather, though.

Prices A beer costs 1000kr to 1800kr, depending on location. Expect to pay upwards of 2000kr for a long drink or cocktail.

REYKJAVÍK EXPERIENCES

On a normal weekend night downtown is teeming with life, with partygoers flocking hither and thither as they migrate from one bar or club to the next. You'll find the different subclasses of partygoers, naturally, at different times throughout the evening and night. We'll give you some ideas that, depending on your clubbing and bar-hopping preferences and whether or not you're in for the full experience, you'll find useful on your prowl.

Food & Drink: 5pm to 11pm

Do you enjoy a happy-hour beer and a meaningful conversation, or perhaps a glass of wine in good company with lively discussion? There are plenty of comfortable sit-downs with good atmosphere around and even some really nice spots for sitting outside if weather permits. If you'd like a little sustenance with

🎵 Gaukur á stöng

A pub and live-music venue, **Gaukurinn** has been home to many Icelandic musicians. More recently, it's also become a haven to the LGBTQI+/alternative/drag scene.

Top left Prikid **Top right** Reykjavik cityscape at dusk **Left** Live performance at Gaukurinn.

your drinks, check out **Kex Hostel**, **Skál!** at Hlemmur Food Court and **Port 9**. Otherwise, **Veður**, **Tíu Sopar** and **Bodega** are great places for drinks and company. In good weather Bodega is highly recommended, as it extends into the square where it's located.

11pm & Onwards

Many Icelanders don't venture out until closer to midnight and prefer partying into the night over the alternative. **Prikið** is one of the oldest bar-cafes in Reykjavík and is a staple of the Icelandic bar and club scene, which during weekends is packed tight by guests. There's little space, but that doesn't stop the crowd from dancing to the beats laid down by that evening's DJ. Prikið is welcoming and cross-generational, but in the late evenings during the weekends it's mostly crammed by under-30s. **Röntgen** is a little more recent and has taken part of the overflow from Prikið, mainly those who are over 30. It's also a

🍾 The Day After

A curated hangover day by our resident creature of the night.

01 Carb up at Grái Kötturinn (Grey Cat); American pancakes and coffee until 2pm.

02 Walk to Grandi; let the sea breeze heal your wrecked nerves.

03 Take an afternoon nap in the park by the Einar Jónsson Museum if weather permits.

04 Down a Gleym-mér-ei burger and a peach schnapps at Vitabar for dinner.

05 Swim in the evening at Sundhöllin swimming pool. Nothing like soaking in a hot-pot with the locals.

Arnar Ingi *Graphic designer, musician and resident creature of the night.*

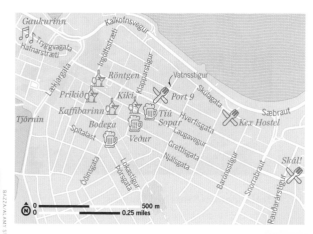

late-night bar-club and has a similar vibe to Prikið, though it's a bit more refined. The DJs read the crowd well, playing anything from electro to funk.

A Deeper Dive

The clock is ticking ever closer to 2am. Heading home might be a good idea, but perhaps you're longing for a deeper dive. Both Prikið and Röntgen are good spots to keep going, but at this hour a few others are coming into their prime, including two major players worth a special mention:

Kaffibarinn This bar has been a prime location for the deep divers of the Reykjavík nightlife for over 25 years. It's remained rowdy, crowded and sweaty forever, and it feels like it's always open. It's the kind of place you might enter for a quiet coffee in the afternoon, only to find yourself stumbling home 14 hours later. It has a long list of regulars from the neighbourhood, but welcomes non-regulars and tourists alike.

Kiki The heart of the local LGBTQI+ scene, but inclusive and approachable to everyone, Kiki is a bar that turns into a nightclub. It's tuned high in terms of party amplitude, plenty of dancing and cheerful intimacy under the beat of various great Icelandic DJs, playing all sorts of music. This is absolutely the place to lose yourself in until morning.

Left Grái Kötturinn (Grey Cat) **Below** Kiki queer bar in Laugavegur

A Brief Take on Icelandic Craft Beer

INFUSING CRAFT BREW WITH LOCAL FLAVOURS

On 1 March 1989, after a prohibition that lasted 74 years, the purchase of beer became legal in Iceland. Until then neither bars, the alcohol monopoly nor anyone else could sell beer. Hence beer was a rarity and contraband. Today the 1st of March is celebrated in Iceland as 'Beer Day'.

Icelanders in Search of Choices

After 1989 two major beverage giants produced and supplied Iceland with beer for over 17 years, until a couple in North Iceland, Agnes and Ólafur, started a brewery of their own, **Bruggsmiðjan Kaldi**, claiming the title of the first craft brewery in Iceland. A few years later, in 2010, a small group of dedicated beer enthusiasts formed a home-brewers club. Their aim was to learn how to brew beer and to create a supply chain to import the necessary ingredients into the country, and in so doing violate yet another prohibition remnant: the ban on home brewing.

In the same period, three craft breweries had been formed: **Ölvisholt**, **Mjöður** and **Gæðingur**. Since then the number of craft breweries has grown rapidly. At the time of writing, there are 27 established craft-beer breweries in Iceland. A majority of those were established in 2017 or later.

What Makes Beer Icelandic?

Iceland isn't a great agricultural source for beer making. What little barley and wheat are grown here are in limited supply, very hardy and not a great source of starch. Furthermore, no malting takes place in Iceland, so in order to use those grains the brewers would need to mix in imported grains or use additional enzymes. For this reason most grains for beer making, and hops of course, are imported from abroad. Then there's Iceland's water, which though crisp and clear lacks the minerals for optimal beer making, and so the minerals you'd normally find in water abroad need to be added too. So what makes beer Icelandic?

Left Main distillation area, Ægisgarður craft beer factory **Middle** Kaldi beer **Right** Gæðingur Microbar

Breweries have taken various approaches to Icelandifying beer. **Og Natura**, for example, uses Icelandic herbs and berries in its products, pairing them with hops in a most inventive manner. **Álfur** uses potato discards, from a local potato manufacturer, as a source of starch mixed in with the wheats and barley. **RVK Brewing Co** puts an entire Christmas tree into the boil for an added spirit of festivities. **Steðji** makes a beer that's spiked with literal whale testicles. **Ölverk** uses geothermal heat to do their mash and boil, and many breweries employ the local *skyr* (yoghurt-style delicacy) to start a lacto-fermentation in kettle-soured beers, adding a very recognisable flavour.

> So what makes beer Icelandic? Breweries have taken various approaches to Icelandifying beer...

So what are you waiting for? There are plenty of brewery taprooms all around Iceland and a variety of craft-beer pubs in downtown Reykjavík.

The Reykjavík Scene

Downtown and the Old Harbour are home to a number of craft bars and breweries with taprooms. Among them are **RVK Brewing Co** and **Honkytonk BBQ**, **Bastard**, **Brewdog Reykjavík**, **Ægir Brewery**, **Skúli Craft Bar**, **Session** and more. If you're willing to venture a little further, you may find yourself in **Gæðingur Microbar** or the **Malbygg** taproom, where the brewers themselves will gladly pour you a pint or five.

🍺 The Monopoly on Alcohol

The Icelandic government retains a monopoly on the retail sale of alcoholic beverages in Iceland through their countrywide stores called Vínbúðin (the alcohol store). It is illegal for private companies to sell alcohol in any shape or form in Iceland. This has been a contentious issue in Iceland for years, and some companies have started selling alcohol via web stores anyway, challenging the government and claiming the laws are unjust since companies outside Icelandic jurisdiction are allowed to sell and distribute to Iceland. So far they remain in business, but only time will tell how this issue is resolved.

03 Culture
NIGHT

FESTIVAL | DOWNTOWN | MUSIC

████ Culture Night, first held in 1996 as a birthday celebration for the city of Reykjavík, is easily the biggest single event in Iceland, with over a third of the population of Iceland attending on a yearly basis.

ARCTIC IMAGES/ALAMY STOCK PHOTO ©

🗺 How to

What Culture Night is a huge collection of simultaneous cultural events.

Where Culture Night is held 'downtown' in the wide sense of the word, with the festival area extending west and east of downtown as well.

When The event generally takes place on the first Saturday after 18 August.

Price The festival is open to everyone, but particular events within the festival may charge for participation.

ARCTIC IMAGES/ALAMY STOCK PHOTO ©

REYKJAVÍK EXPERIENCES

Culture Night During the Day

Particular locations and events have with time become staples of the festival, but by far the largest part of it is independently organised and executed by various individuals and groups, so each festival is mostly comprised of 'wildcard' events. Many of them go on the schedule, but others don't, so keep an eye out! Just walking around, not least in the residential areas of downtown, will surely bring you to flea markets, independent art exhibitions, home concerts and...waffles.

The city gives so-called 'waffle grants' to residents who are willing to accept hundreds of guests into their homes or into their gardens and serve them waffles all day long. The mayor at the time of writing, has personally baked waffles in the thousands for guests in his own home. Another staple event is the Reykjavík

ARCTIC IMAGES/GETTY IMAGES ©

☼ Planning Your Day

A glossary of events and activities can be found on the festival website (menningar-nott.is). It's the best source of information to plan your day. Take into consideration that there will be over 100,000 people in town, so travel times will be longer than normal.

Top left A choir entertains the crowd **Top right** Aerial silks performance **Left** The Reykjavík Marathon begins

Marathon. It is the first event of the day and generally has around 10,000 participants from Iceland and all over the world. Runners can choose five different distances to run, ranging from 600m to the marathon.

What to Expect During the Day

On a stroll through town you'll find a variety of diversions. Events vary from year to year, but in years past have included a bread-cake-decorating competition at the Reykjavík Art Museum, a street-food convention by the harbour, dance exhibitions, tightly packed events at the art galleries, backyard concerts, a silent disco at the library, a guided tour through the art collections of the downtown bank, poetry readings, an interactive VR theatre experience for one, and numerous street performances.

The Evening

Dinner may need a bit of planning if you're hoping to grab a table, so book in advance.

☸ Tips from the Mayor

01 Start the day by participating in the Reykjavík Marathon. You can run the shorter distances, it does not matter, but it is a great way to experience the city from street level, go into neighbourhoods and run by the ocean. And you start the day with endorphins in your veins.

02 Go with the flow. Be welcomed into people's homes or experience music in a backyard. There are interesting things going on everywhere. Go for the unplanned and unexpected.

03 Attend the numerous concerts during the evening, and end the night watching the dancing fireworks in the sky.

Dagur B Eggertsson *mayor of Reykjavík. @Dagurb*

ARCTIC-IMAGES/GETTY IMAGES ©

Far left Fireworks light up the city
Left A crowd gathers on Arnarhóll hill
Below Boy eating waffle

However, many restaurants will have food-related events throughout the day and early evening, so you'll probably be able to refuel on the go. The final big event of the day is a concert at Arnarhóll hill where each year a diverse cast of performers entertain a crowd. It generally starts around 8pm. Slowly but surely the hill and surrounding areas fill with people. As the concert comes to a close at around 11pm, it culminates in a countdown in which everyone participates, chanting and anticipating one of the biggest fireworks displays of the year (perhaps beaten only by the chaotic battering of fireworks on New Year's Eve). Following the fireworks most people head home, and the Reykjavík nightlife takes over. What you decide to do next is a whole other chapter.

ARCTIC-IMAGES/GETTY IMAGES ©

04 A Capital of
CULTURE

ART | HISTORY | CULTURE

Reykjavík was designated one of the European capitals of culture in the year 2000. For good reason too, as Reykjavík's heritage, cultural institutions and independently run spaces are both plentiful and diverse.

SIGURÐUR ARNI SIGURÐSSON, EXPANSE, 2020 © REYKJAVÍK ART MUSEUM

🗺 How to

Getting around Most of the locations are in, or close to, downtown. For more distant places, a car or the city bus are the best modes of transport.

When to go Year-round, though for outdoor cultural spots it's ideal to aim for late spring, summer or early fall. Or any time the weather decides to be less antagonistic.

Prices The Reykjavík City Card will save you money if you're planning a cultural day or three.

STOCKCAM/GETTY IMAGES ©

REYKJAVÍK EXPERIENCES

Downtown & Around

The city of Reykjavík plays host to many of the country's cultural institutions, and for the most part, they're located downtown or within walking distance of it. It should be easy to compose a full day or two of cultural exploration.

Reykjavík Art Museum, with its collections of local artists and emphasis on 21st-century art, is an integral part of the capital's art scene. Displayed over three locations – Hafnarhús, Kjarvalsstaðir and Ásmundarsafn – all can be visited with the same ticket of admission. Hafnarhús is the largest and most central of the locations. An ideal day trip could be visiting them in this order and ending your day by bathing in Laugardalslaug, which is conveniently close by Ásmundarsafn.

DAN SHACHAR/SHUTTERSTOCK ©

ⓘ Reykjavík City Card

The Reykjavík City Card (visitreykjavik.is) grants you admission to all of the museums and exhibitions run by the city, plus the swimming pools and the city bus too! It can be purchased in one- to three-day variants.

Top left Reykjavík Art Museum, Kjarvalsstaðir **Top right** View of Hafnarfjörður, home to Hafnarborg **Left** Medieval wood church door, National Museum of Iceland

There are plenty of cultural locations in downtown and vicinity. The **National Gallery of Iceland** by the pond is responsible for the art that's nationally owned and houses a variety of events and exhibitions of art from the 20th and 21st centuries. The **Einar Jónsson Museum** and sculpture garden is located next to the landmark Hallgrímskirkja and is dedicated to the art of Einar Jónsson, Iceland's first sculptor. Even when the museum is closed, the garden is a worthwhile excursion:

it's great for picnics! The **National Museum of Iceland** is also only a short walk from downtown and offers a fantastic glimpse into how Iceland got to where it is today. It houses both permanent and temporary exhibitions with audio tours available in many languages.

Off the Beaten Path

Reykjavík is obviously bigger than just downtown and its surrounds. Some days you simply might want to explore a little more.

Art in Public Spaces

Þúfan (Tussock), by Ólöf Nordal A significant landmark in the cityscape. The *Tussock* is a taunt as it's not local to cities: it's a pest in farming and constructing one is essentially an oxymoron.

Áfangar, by Richard Serra An unusual work by the artist, as *Áfangar* is made of basalt. Located on Viðey island, it deals with height contours in the Icelandic landscape.

The Tree of Signs, by Gabríela Friðriksdóttir Located far from the beaten path for a traveller, it's visible from the local IKEA and Costco but is simultaneously in seemingly untouched nature.

Harpa Þórsdóttir *director of The National Gallery of Iceland.*

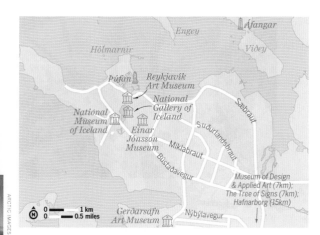

Left Kópavogslaug **Below** Reykjavík Art Museum, Hafnarhús

In the town of Hafnarfjörður, south of Reykjavík, you can visit **Hafnarborg**, which houses the town's art collection. There are rotating exhibitions of both modern and contemporary works by various artists from the museum archives, as well as guest exhibitors. It's absolutely worth a visit in combination with a nice exploration of the old town of Hafnarfjörður, built on the edge of an old lava field and the sea.

Kópavogur, another Reykjavík neighbour, has its own cultural institution called **Gerðarsafn**. It's no less a beautiful building to visit than an interesting museum for discovering Icelandic modern and contemporary art. On top of that it's located right next to the main transport hub of Kópavogur, and has a very good outdoor area for picnics and children. Close by the museum is the **Kópavogslaug swimming pool**, easily one of the best pools for children.

The **Museum of Design and Applied Art** is located on Garðatorg square, in adjacent municipality Garðabær, and has exhibitions in various different design categories. Perhaps a hidden gem if you're willing to make the trip.

HRAUN/GETTY IMAGES ©

🎵♪

A Path to Musical Excellence?

LOCAL SOUNDS, GLOBAL AUDIENCES

Iceland has produced many globally known musicians. Whether that number is the highest per capita, as many Icelanders proudly proclaim, is debatable. Regardless, given Iceland's size, the extent of the musical footprint it has left on global consciousness is extraordinary.

Starting Early

It's common in Iceland for parents to send their children to choirs from an early age. Once children start school, other options open up, such as learning classical instruments at music schools or getting lessons in primary school. Lessons prepare kids to participate in school bands, and these bands expose them to a variety of instruments. Alongside this, the children take obligatory music lessons in school where they learn the basics of music and creation and cooperation, and get exposed to the musical heritage of Iceland and other cultures.

Creating Platforms

Part of running a successful nationwide music program is creating the platforms from which bands and musicians can launch.

Tónlistarþróunarmiðstöðin The Centre for Music Development, run by an old Icelandic punk legend, is a place where bands can get rooms to keep their equipment and practice their craft. Furthermore, it organises events at which the bands can perform.

Músíktilraunir At this event, bands from across Iceland compete annually in front of a live audience. Among the bands to feature in the competition are Sigur Rós, Mammút, Of Monsters and Men, RetRoBoT (Daði Freyrs band before he went solo), Vök, Samaris, and Agent Fresco.

Iceland Airwaves The biggest music festival in Iceland hosts performances from local and overseas talent. Alongside the festival is a brilliant off-venue program crowded with upcoming names on the Icelandic music scene.

Left Teenager playing the trombone **Middle** Musical performance **Right** Nanna Bryndís Hilmarsdóttir, Of Monsters and Men on stage.

The Present

Sigtryggur Baldursson, musician and managing director of the Iceland Music Export Office, is optimistic about the future of Icelandic music. His dream scenario is a music scene where musicians can make a living without being household names. To this end, he's been involved in a project that creates guides for young musicians about managing their career and their rights, among other things.

> Although Icelandic music has come to be identified with the ethereal sound of internationally recognised performers... they're not the totality of Icelandic music.

Although Icelandic music has come to be identified with the ethereal sound of internationally recognised performers such as Sigur Rós, Hjaltalín and Björk, they're not the totality of Icelandic music. You might be familiar with bands and musical projects without realising they're Icelandic. Did you know, for instance, that Of Monsters and Men, Kaleo and GusGus are Icelandic bands?

Baldursson says that bands that become popular locally face a tough choice: while there may be enough work available in Iceland for bands to survive, to grow they may need to operate from abroad.

So what's the best way to get acquainted with Icelandic music? Baldursson recommends the Spotify playlist at icelandicmusic.is. Furthermore, if you're looking for events, the gig list in the Reykjavík Grapevine (grapevine.is) is the go-to list for concerts.

♫♪ Girls Rock!

The Girls Rock camp is a project that originated in the USA with the goal of instigating social change by creating a platform for girls, women and trans/non-binary people to take space in popular music culture where they are severely under-represented. This project also took flight in Iceland and is now actively recruiting girls and hatching new bands en masse. The programs are mostly run for children and teenagers, but they also have occasional programs for adults. What's remarkable is that no prior music experience is required; the goal is to create new opportunities, after all.

05 Urban **HIKING**

WALKS | NATURE | CATS

Put on your good shoes, pack your swimsuit, visit the nichest museum in Iceland, see the first settlements, smell the sea and bathe with locals. Oh, and don't forget to pet the cats of Reykjavík.

STEPHEN BRIDGER /SHUTTERSTOCK ©

🗺 Trip Notes

How long? This walk, while only about 4km long, can easily take a whole day with the activities suggested.

Tips Bring a swimsuit and dress according to the weather. On the way there are plenty of good places to stop for lunch.

Costs The entry fee for the Phallological Museum is 2500kr, the Settlement Exhibition 1800kr and the pool 1060kr.

🐾 Cats of Reykjavík

Perhaps the true locals of Reykjavík, cats are everywhere and it can be fun to keep that in mind when walking around. They are popular as pets in Iceland and generally get to roam freely – a bother to some and celebrated by others. Cat patrols can be spotted wherever you go.

05 You packed a swimsuit and fresh socks, right? That wasn't for the beach! Sit back, relax and converse with the locals about the news and the weather in **Vesturbæjarlaug** swimming pool.

02 Icelandic Phallological Museum displays penises from over 100 species of mammals, including a human and, supposedly, a specimen from hidden folk, more commonly known as elves.

OLD REYKJAVÍK

Túngata · Pósthússtræti · Kalkofnsvegur · Lækjargata · Hverfisgata · Laugavegur · Sæbraut

Hofsvallagata · Hagamelur · Hringbraut · Tjörnin · Skólavörðustígur · Bergþórugata

Melhagi · Neshagi

MELAR

Fornhagi · Dunhagi · Suðurgata · Sóleyjargata · Barónsstígur · Snorrabraut · Raudarárstígur

Ægissíða · Starhagi

03 During building work in 2001, a well-preserved settlement partly dating back to the year 871 was discovered. A **Settlement Exhibition** was ingeniously integrated into the building being worked on.

01 The Protestant church of **Hallgrímskirkja** was until recently the tallest building in Reykjavík. It's construction started in 1945, and it wasn't formally opened until 1986.

04 Visit the seafront, explore the sloppy kelp jungles of **Ægissíða** and have a stroll around the old fishing sheds of **Grímsstaðavör**. Ægissíða is a popular path and beach to walk along and enjoy.

Reykjavík 871 ±2 · Landnámssýningin The Settlement Exhibition

N

0 — 1 km
0 — 0.5 miles

Listings

BEST OF THE REST

Craft Beer

Brewdog

Brewdog is located in a side street off Laugavegur. In addition to its ambitious selection of Icelandic craft beer its staff and attitude is top-notch.

Microbar

Located close to the central bus station in Kópavogur, Microbar is the new location of the first true craft bar in Iceland. Cosy but off the beaten path.

Session

Perhaps the new gold standard for craft bars in Iceland, Session always has a great variety and plenty of beer-related events. Great location on the main shopping street.

Skúli Craft Bar

A charismatic little craft bar next to Ingólfstorg downtown. Great location and atmosphere and a good bottle list.

Malbygg Taproom

Malbygg is the cool kid of the Icelandic brewery scene. Its taproom is stocked with its own beers and plenty of imports. The location in Skútuvogur is tough to reach.

RVK Brewing Taproom

Ten minutes' walk from Hlemmur food court. Its small taproom has a good view into the brewery.

Ægir Taproom

At the far end of Grandi (the Old Harbour) lies Ægir Brewery. Check that it's open before you go.

Restaurants

Dill   €€€€

The only Michelin-starred restaurant in Iceland. It works hard to make your experience unique while maintaining a sustainable approach. Downtown location.

Public House   €€

Located on Laugavegur, Public House is a reasonably priced downtown restaurant with a nice approach to Icelandic–Japanese fusion. Also, it has a peephole...

ÓX   €€€€

A small speakeasy spot, hidden behind Sumac restaurant. It's more of a dining experience than a traditional restaurant. Few seats available, so book ahead.

Austur Indíafélagið   €€€

Fancy Indian food? This is as authentic as you can get it in Iceland. Prime downtown location and a simple and relaxing interior.

Dragon Dim Sum   €€

Dragon Dim Sum is a recent addition to the

Reykjavík City Library

restaurant scene and has quickly become the go-to place for dumplings/dim sum. Good location in a side street off Laugavegur.

 ## Quick Bites

Mandi   €

Situated in the heart of downtown, Mandi is perfect for a post-drink bite.

Vitabar   €

You've had a long Saturday night and you're craving a sloppy burger. Vitabar on Vitastígur, downtown, has you covered.

 ## Art & Culture

Punk Museum

Right downtown there's a stairway into the sidewalk where Frikki Punk runs an exhibition dedicated to Iceland's punk scene.

I8

A gallery located downtown, I8 has exhibitions by current art powerhouses, both Icelandic and from abroad. A must-visit for the visual-arts-oriented travellers.

Reykjavík City Library

The library's main building sits downtown. In addition to its customary function, it's home to concerts, culture walks, poetry readings and the Icelandic Photography Museum.

 ## History

Árbæjarsafn

The open-air museum is a collection of old buildings and a vision of life in the olden days. Visit one of the turf houses and have a taste of homemade pastry.

Viðey

Originally an active volcano, then a significant location in Icelandic history and now a

Árbæjarsafn open-air museum

glorious place to enjoy geology, birds, history and art all in one place. Grab a ferry to Viðey!

 ## Public Parks & Outdoors

Klambratún

Klambratún park is a five-minute walk from Hlemmur food court. It's home to part of the Reykjavík Art Museum and a perfectly good Frisbee golf course. Great for picnics!

Elliðaárdalur

Elliðaárdalur is the biggest green area in the capital region. It's home to birds and is one of the few areas where wild rabbits reside. Easily accessible by bus.

Hvaleyrarvatn

Take a short hike around this small lake and its pretty environment, including a large woodlands area. Close by it's possible to go horseback riding with Íshestar.

Grótta

Grótta is the tip of the Reykjavík peninsula. It has a lighthouse and is thrillingly close to the sea. There's a warm pool to dip your feet into.

 Scan to find more things to do in Reykjavík online

SNEHIT PHOTO/SHUTTERSTOCK ©

REYKJAVÍK REVIEWS

Esjan

A bus ride away, Esjan is a pretty tall mountain considering it's next door to Reykjavík. It has great views, facilities and walking paths. See Reykjavík from across the bay.

Petting Zoo

Do you like sheep? In Laugardalur you can find the only zoo in Iceland where you can meet those exotic animals and many more in person! Actually way more fun than it sounds.

Öskjuhlíð

Cycle or wander the paths that wind through these pine and birch woodlands close to the city centre.

Heiðmörk

This suburban open space on the edge of the city is great for walking among Sitka spruce and the Rauðhólar (Red Hills), a volcanic area that's part of the Elliðaárhraun lava field.

≋ Swimming Pools

Sundhöllin

The city's oldest swimming pool is located downtown. It has been upgraded to modern standards. Has an outdoor swimming pool and hot tubs.

Vesturbæjarlaug

A 25m outdoor swimming pool, a children's pool and hot tubs. Close by is an ice-cream parlour, a cafe and a fast-food diner.

Kópavogslaug

A 50m outdoor swimming pool, nice hot tubs, slides and an indoor swimming pool. This pool is in the next town over from Reykjavík, but is easily accessed by bus.

Salalaug

A 25m outdoor swimming pool with a few hot tubs and a fun slide for the children. Salalaug is in Kópavogur, easily reached by bus or car.

Lágafellslaug

Sports a 25m swimming pool, hot tubs and three slides outside and an indoor swimming pool for the kids. Located in Mosfellsbær, on the way in or out of the city.

Nauthólsvík

Nauthólsvík geothermal beach is a half-hour walk from downtown or five minutes by bus. How about lying in the tub or bathing in the North Atlantic?

Music Venues

Harpa

Harpa Concert Centre is located harbourside in downtown. It's architecture is the pride of Reykjavík, and it's home to various events and the symphonic orchestra.

KEX Hostel

At KEX Hostel, downtown, there are often concerts in the evenings featuring artists that are up-and-coming or known entities in Iceland.

Mengi

Mengi is a venue operated by artists; it hosts diverse music and art events. It's located in a prime location downtown and its schedule is progressive.

A trail in Esjan

◎ Other Attractions

Tjarnarbíó

Tjarnarbíó theatre, the cinema by the pond, has a variety of shows on its calendar, plus plays (some performed in English), contemporary dance, concerts and more.

Kolaportið Flea Market

Kolaportið (the coal storage) is the only flea market in Iceland. It's open on weekends and is definitely worth a visit.

Fly over Iceland

In Grandi you can experience flying over Iceland in a state-of-the-art cinema. It offers motion, curved cinema, wind, smell – immersive cinema like you've never experienced before.

Whales of Iceland

Right next to Fly over Iceland you can visit the whales. Walk among life-sized models of 23 types of whales.

Wonders of Iceland

Wonders of Iceland

In Perlan, a landmark building in Reykjavík, you can experience the sounds of earthquakes, visit Látrabjarg cliff in augmented reality, walk through an actual ice cave and see the aurora in Iceland's only planetarium.

REYKJAVÍK REVIEWS

THE GOLDEN CIRCLE

NATIONAL PARKS | WATERFALLS | GEOTHERMAL SPRINGS

Experience
the Golden
Circle online

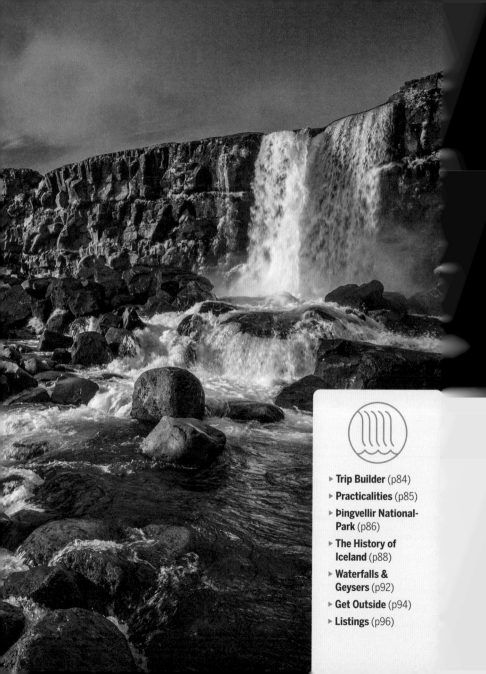

THE GOLDEN CIRCLE
Trip Builder

Langjökull

The Golden Circle tourist route can be completed in a day. Its main sights include Þingvellir, Geysir and Gullfoss, but the region is also packed with hidden-gem waterfalls, important historical sites and unique geological landscapes.

Marvel at **Gullfoss**, a cascading two-tiered waterfall that drops into a ravine (p93)
🕐 *1 hour*

Haukadalur

Brattholt

○ Brúarhlöð

▲ *Þingvellir National Park*

○ Skálabrekka

Laugarvatn ○
Laugarvatn

▲ *Efstadalsfjall*

Golden Circle

Apavatn

Þingvallavatn

Watch the geyser spout water up to 40m into the air at **Geysir** (p93)
🕐 *1 hour*

Walk between the North American and Eurasian tectonic plates at **Þingvellir** (p86)
🕐 *1 hour*

○ Skálholt

Flúðir ○

Ölfusá

Soak in the **Secret Lagoon**, an outdoor natural hot spring pool (p97)
🕐 *1–2 hours*

Walk the rim of **Kerið,** a colorful volcanic crater filled with bright blue water (p95)
🕐 *1 hour*

Explore bookable experiences in the Golden Circle online

Ⓝ 0 ___ 10 km
0 ___ 5 miles

Practicalities

ARRIVING

Keflavík International Airport
All international flights come and go through this airport, 89km from Þingvellir. The drive from Reykjavík is short and the roads are good. Buses depart regularly from Reykjavík.

FIND YOUR WAY

There's a tourist-information centre at Þingvellir National Park.

MONEY

Debit/credit cards are widely accepted. You'll pay for parking at Þingvellir and Kerið, and for toilets at Þingvellir and Gullfoss.

WHERE TO STAY

Town	Pro/Con
Laugarvatn	Has quaint guesthouses for those who don't want to complete the entire Circle in one day.
Flúðir	Detour to overnight at a B&B and soak in nearby hot springs.
Selfoss	Abundant hotels and guesthouses and a good location to continue onto the South Coast.

GETTING AROUND

Car Driving is the best way to explore places off the beaten path.

Tour bus For those who want to sit back and take it all in.

Private tour Let someone handle the planning details.

EATING & DRINKING

Geothermal bakery Eat rye bread that was baked using geothermal energy at Laugarvatn (p96).

Best tomato-themed menu Friðheimar (p96)

Must-try ice cream Efstidalur (p96)

APR–MAY
Cooler temperatures, brown landscapes.

JUN–AUG
Everything is green, fair temperatures, midnight sun.

SEP–OCT
Rain and wind is very common.

NOV–MAR
Snowy with limited daylight hours.

06 Þingvellir National PARK

HISTORY | TECTONIC PLATES | OUTDOORS

Þingvellir is a Unesco World Heritage Site for its history and geological elements. Here you will find multiple fissures caused by the rifting of the North American and Eurasian tectonic plates. It's also the site of the Alþingi, Iceland's democratic parliament established in 930 CE.

STOCKPHOTOS2/GETTY IMAGES ©

🗺 How to

Getting here Rent a car, take the bus or join a guided tour.

When to go To avoid crowds, skip the park between 10am and 11am when the tour buses come through.

Parking Multiple lots around the park for 750kr to 1000kr depending on vehicle size.

Amenities The visitor centre has an interactive history and nature exhibit. The cafe offers coffee and food. Gift shop too.

VENTURA/SHUTTERSTOCK ©

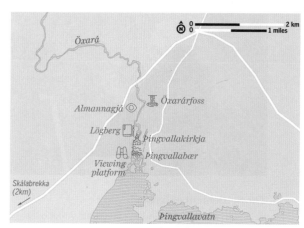

Top Rift inside Pingvellir National Park
Bottom Þingvallakirkja

Iceland sits directly on the boundary between the North American and Eurasian tectonic plates, which runs through Þingvellir. These plates are spreading apart at a rate of 2.5cm per year, which reveals cracks and canyons in the landscape.

Viewing platform Near the main parking lot sits a large platform that overlooks the entire park, including Þingvallavatn, the largest natural lake in Iceland.

Almannagjá The official rift where you can walk between continents. The walls of the ridge are made up of the North American and Eurasian tectonic plates to the west and east, respectively.

Þingvallabær Translates to 'Þingvellir town', made up of five houses that are now used as the park warden's office and the prime minister's summer house.

Þingvallakirkja Just past the houses is the church of Þingvellir. It's usually closed, but opens around 10am for a guided tour from the park ranger.

Lögberg The approximate location of where parliament gathered. It translates to 'Law Rock', which is where the speaker would stand to make announcements during gatherings. Today the Icelandic flag stands in its spot.

Öxarárfoss At the end of the Almannagjá rift, a beautiful waterfall cascades over the cliff of the North American plate into a river gorge.

The Bloody Gate *Game of Thrones* fans will recognise one of the Almannagjá canyons as a filming location from the show.

🦿 Around Þingvellir

Enhance your time at Þingvellir by adding an activity or tour around the area. Hikers can stop in the visitor centre for a map of multiple trails of varying distances around the park, while local tour operators conduct tours of the area on horseback. There are also water-based activities: you can angle for trout and char in the clear cold waters of lake Þingvallavatn, or the cold-resistant can snorkel or dive between continents in crystal-clear glacier water (p95). The area around lake Þingvallavatn is also a great place for birdwatching and spotting mink or Arctic foxes, Iceland's only native mammal.

WANDERLUSTER/GETTY IMAGES ©

The History of Iceland

ICELAND'S POLITICAL HISTORY LOCATED BETWEEN TECTONIC PLATES

To Icelanders Þingvellir is more than simply the place where tectonic plates split apart. Literally meaning 'assembly plains', Þingvellir was once a gathering place for major historical events and is now a national shrine and Unesco World Heritage Site.

Left Viking reenactor, Þingvellir
Middle Þingvellir landscape **Right** Cliffs of the continental fault, Þingvellir

The Settlement of Iceland

Iceland is unusual in that it was settled late. Around the year 870 there were no permanent inhabitants of Iceland. As kingdoms developed in the Middle Ages, the Norwegian king was known for being overbearing, so a lot of powerful landowners wanted to move and make new settlements. Norwegian seafarers headed west and found new land to settle. Ingólfur Arnarson is known to be the first settler on the island. When Iceland became known, Scandinavians started migrating via boat. There was never a king or executive authority, but rather a decentralised and wide-spread distribution of power. For that to work, the people came together once a year to form a national assembly, or Alþingi, held at Þingvellir.

Founding the Parliament

In the Middle Ages, Iceland didn't have towns or cities. Landowners were powerful as they owned land and slaves. Once the land was fully settled, locals needed to establish a way of governing themselves to counterbalance the growing power of a small number of landowners. District assemblies were formed in the beginning, but as the population grew it became apparent that a general assembly was needed. So in 930 Þingvellir was established, and parliament remained there for hundreds of years.

Annual Assemblies

Due to accessibility as well as an abundance of fresh water and forests, Þingvellir was chosen as the meeting

location. People from all regions of Iceland would travel for days to arrive at the annual assembly. The powerful regional leaders known as *goði* came together to make decisions. Once there, everyone would build booths out of stone, turf and cloth. It was the biggest event of the year and reminiscent of a festival, with attendees entertaining one another.

At the centre of the assembly plains was a structure known as Lögberg (Law Rock). Anyone could stand at Lögberg and give a speech on matters they found important. It was here that news was reported, information was exchanged, conflicts were resolved and marriages were arranged.

> There was never a king or executive authority, but rather a decentralised and widespread distribution of power.

The Law Speaker

It was the law speaker, elected by the *goði* chieftains, who held the power at these meetings. Around the year 1000, the country was divided between pagans and the new religion of Christianity. The law speaker at that time had to decide what to do about the new religion. He hid under a cloak for a day to meditate on the decision. When he emerged, he stated 'We are one land and one people so we should have one law' and peacefully decided on Christianity with three caveats: can still worship in private, can still eat horse meat and can still expose unwanted children. Today, an Icelandic flag stands in the spot where the Law Rock was thought to be.

Heart of Iceland

Inside the visitor centre at Þingvellir National Park, you'll find the newly opened *Heart of Iceland*, an interactive exhibit that beautifully portrays the history and nature of Þingvellir and why it means so much to Icelanders. Using state-of-the-art technology, it allows you to reveal artefacts from the area, trace the routes locals travelled to get to the annual assembly, and visualise the law counsel and what went on at the meetings. Also learn how water travels from the glacier through filtered lava rock and into nearby lake Þingvallavatn, and what the future of Þingvellir holds.

Admission adult/child 1000kr/free.

DELPIXEL/SHUTTERSTOCK ©

The Present Day

The national assembly continued meeting at Þingvellir until 1798 when it was moved to Reykjavík. In 1930, Þingvellir became Iceland's first national park, and in 2004 it was listed as a Unesco World Heritage Site. Today Þingvellir looks the same as it always has: aside from the pathways to accommodate tourism, you're standing on a field that has always been a field, the site of the annual meeting, and one the biggest parts of the nation's history.

> In 1930, Þingvellir became Iceland's first national park, and in 2004 it was listed as a Unesco World Heritage Site.

With thanks to Dale Kedwards, who researches medieval Icelandic culture at the Árni Magnússon Institute for Icelandic Studies. dalekedwards.com.

📖 Þingvellir Sagas

The sagas are an important part of Icelandic heritage. Written in the 13th century about events occurring between the 9th and 13th centuries, these books recount the struggles and conflicts during the settlement era. Many of the sagas take place at Þingvellir. Topics include the settlement, geological events, famine, witchcraft and bloody battles. For those interested in reading the sagas, there's further reading online (sagadb.org).

While the sagas were written some 200 years after the actual events took place, it is known that exaggerations can be found in the writings. Icelanders embrace this, as it makes the stories that much more entertaining. Nevertheless, the sagas are important documents of courage, perseverance and what life was like at the time.

Left Þingvellir **Above left** Detail of Iceland Manuscript containing Icelandic sagas **Above right** Iceland's flag flies at what is thought to be the location of Lögberg (Law Rock)

07 Waterfalls & GEYSERS

LANDSCAPES | NATURE | HIDDEN GEMS

Water is a common theme in Iceland, whether it's melting from a glacier, cascading over a cliff, or heated with geothermal energy from the ground. Along the Golden Circle you will find all of these elements in a relatively small geographical area.

BILDAGENTUR ZOONAR GMBH/SHUTTERSTOCK ©

🗺 How to

Getting here Rent a car and drive yourself to reach places off the beaten path.

When to go Geysir, Gullfoss and Faxi can be accessed year-round. Brúarfoss should only be attempted between May to October.

What to wear Warm layers and waterproof clothing from head to toe is essential no matter what time of year you're visiting.

PURIPAT LERTPUNYAROJ/SHUTTERSTOCK ©

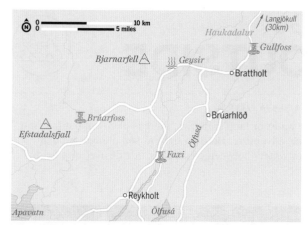

Top Brúarfoss
Bottom Strokkur geyser

The horse's mane Faxi is a small but mighty waterfall just south of Gullfoss. A 700kr parking fee gets you access to this serene oasis. A small cafe and picnic area on-site are good spots to enjoy a midday bite. The surrounding nature is a great spot for birdwatching, and you might even see salmon jumping up the river in the summer.

Geothermal valley Geysir is a geothermal area in the Haukadalur valley that is home to geysers, fumaroles and mud-pits. The main attraction is Strokkur, which erupts up to 40m (131ft) every seven to 10 minutes.

Crown jewel of the Circle Gullfoss translates to 'Golden Falls' and is a double-cascade waterfall dropping 32m into a massive gorge. The water comes from the nearby Langjökull, Iceland's second-largest glacier.

The elusive blue falls Bright-blue water cascading over black lava rock makes **Brúarfoss** waterfall unique. To get there requires a three-hour round-trip hike. There is a designated parking lot off Rte 37 between Þingvellir and Geysir. The trail runs along the river and is easy to follow, and two smaller bonus waterfalls can be found along the way. Note: in April and May the trail gets extremely muddy; from June to October is a great time to tackle this hike; and from November to March the trail is inaccessible.

ⓘ Dress for Adventure

'There's no such thing as bad weather, only bad clothing.' This Icelandic saying might leave some people scratching their head. What's good versus bad clothing is not obvious to everyone, especially if you're not used to rain, high winds and low temperatures. The weather is notoriously unpredictable in Iceland, so proper attire is important, especially when travelling the Golden Circle. Its location away from the coast means it tends to be colder and windier. Wear layers that you can remove or add as conditions change. Sturdy footwear and waterproof outerwear (head to toe) are also critical.

08 Get OUTSIDE

ADVENTURE | SNORKELLING | LAVA FIELDS

Whether you prefer water or land activities, there is plenty of outdoor fun to add to your Golden Circle adventure. Hold on tight as you plunge through glacier rivers, snorkel in icy waters between continents, or ride over lava fields on an Icelandic horse.

NUDIBLUE/GETTY IMAGES ©

🗺 How to

Getting here Drive a rental car, or join an organised tour. Most tour companies are Reykjavík-based and can provide hotel pick-up.

When to go These experiences can be accessed year-round but should be booked in advance.

How much 15,000kr to 25,000kr

What to wear Tour companies will outfit you with the necessary equipment and safety gear. Bring warm layers, sturdy hiking boots and a change of clothes.

KETAN VIKAMSEY/SHUTTERSTOCK ©

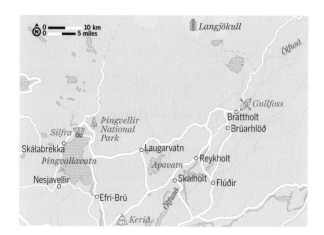

Snorkel between continents Silfra is one of the prominent fissures in Þingvellir National Park, only this one is filled with freezing-cold water. Here you can snorkel (or dive if you're certified) between continents. The water is extremely clear, as it comes from the Langjökull glacier and is filtered through lava rocks. In Silfra, there are no fish or coral, just some bright-green algae and visibility can be up to 100m!

Snowmobile on a glacier Take sightseeing to a whole new level by snowmobiling on top of a glacier. **Langjökull** glacier is Iceland's second-largest ice cap and is located just 30km from Gullfoss waterfall. This unique tour is offered year-round and creates memories for a lifetime.

Paddle through canyons Just below **Gullfoss** waterfall is the canyon that forms the Hvítá river. Get your adrenaline pumping while white-water rafting between volcanic walls. Great for a novice or experienced rafter. It's possible to meet on location or get picked up from Reykjavík. (adventures.is)

Ride over lava fields Take in the landscape on horseback with the adorable Icelandic horse. Known for their short stature and even temperament, the Icelandic horse is an important and beloved part of the culture. They have five gaits – two of which are unique: the *tölt* (running walk) and the flying pace. But don't worry, a riding tour would be a basic slow walk, perfect for adults and children alike.

Top Free diver, Silfra
Bottom Icelandic horses

🚶 Walk a Volcanic Crater

A lesser-known sight along the Golden Circle route is **Kerið**, a volcanic crater lake. This crater, thought to be 6500 years old, is 55m deep and 170m wide. Its vibrant red walls dotted with green moss and filled with turquoise water make it one of the most picturesque places in the country. Walking the crater rim takes about 30 minutes to one hour. On one end of the crater is a pathway to walk down to the water to get a perspective of the crater's size. There's a parking fee of 400kr, which helps the landowner maintain the area.

Listings

BEST OF THE REST

Barns & Greenhouses

Friðheimar €€

Located in the small town of Reykholt, this sustainable and ecofriendly greenhouse has a tomato-themed menu. The most popular dish is the all-you-can-eat tomato soup served with homemade bread. Reservations required.

Efstidalur €

A family-run farm turned into an ice-cream shop and restaurant. Enjoy delicious farm-fresh ice cream while hanging out with the cows. You'll find it just a short drive east of Laugarvatn.

Laugarvatn Geothermal Bakery €

Sample homemade rye bread baked using geothermal energy from the ground. Top it off with Icelandic butter and locally sourced smoked trout.

Flúðasveppir Farmers Bistro €€

Attached to Iceland's only mushroom farm, just outside Flúðir, this restaurant serves mushroom soup with homemade bread and a selection of *álegg* (things that go on bread).

Restaurants

Lindin €€

Midway between Þingvellir and Gullfoss, this could be the best restaurant for miles. It faces the lake and is purely gourmet, with high-concept Icelandic fare featuring local or wild-caught ingredients.

Silfra Restaurant €€€

In the Ion Adventure Hostel on the southern side of Þingvellir National Park, Silfra serves modern Icelandic fare with a Slow Food twist, featuring locally sourced ingredients.

Culture & History

The Cave People

Tour the cave where a nomadic family lived a century ago. Learn about their struggles and what daily life looked like. Enjoy a coffee and an Icelandic treat afterwards. West of Laugarvatn.

Skalholt Cathedral

Historic location for culture, spirituality and music, and the first school to educate clergy was founded here in 1056. Tour the church, crypt, tunnel and archaeological site.

Slakki Petting Zoo

Petting zoo with Arctic foxes, cows, puppies, pigs and more. The zoo also has a minigolf putting course inside a greenhouse.

Búðir

The stone foundations of the *búðir* (literally 'booths') where parliament-goers camped during Alþingi sessions, can still be seen north of the church in Þingvellir.

Grilled lamb filet, Lindin restaurant

Hot Water

Laugarvatn Fontana

Hot spring spa with hot tubs of varying temperatures. Take a dip in the cold lake nearby for the ultimate therapeutic experience.

Secret Lagoon

Oldest constructed pool in Iceland fed by a natural hot spring. The area around the pool consists of mossy lava, geothermal spots and a small bubbling geyser. Near Flúðir.

 Spectacular Stays

Buubble Hotel €€€

Sleep under the stars in a clear bubble tent in the countryside near Reykholt. Recline and watch the midnight sun or, in winter, look for the aurora borealis. A once-in-a-lifetime experience.

Skalholt Cathedral

Hótel Geysir €€

Located right on the doorstep of the geothermal area of Geysir, this four-star hotel is minimalist cool, highlighting its stunning surroundings. For the ultimate induglence, visit the spa.

THE GOLDEN CIRCLE REVIEWS

 Scan to find more things to do in the Golden Circle online

SOUTHWEST ICELAND & REYKJANES PENINSULA

LAVA FIELDS | SEA CLIFFS | GEOTHERMAL

Experience
Southwest
Iceland
online

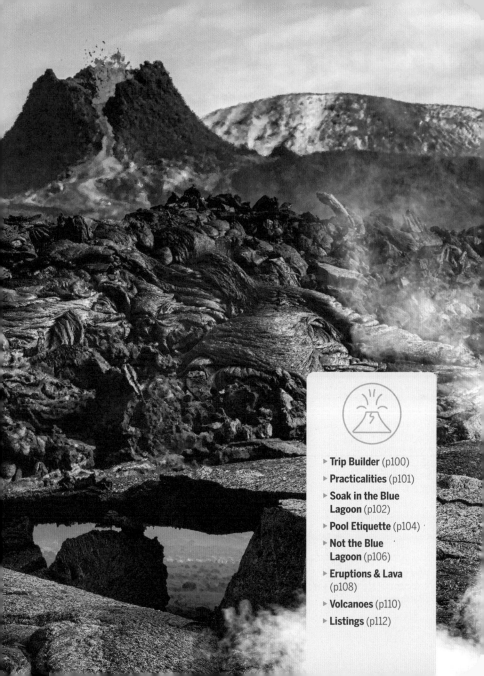

SOUTHWEST ICELAND
Trip Builder

Although most famous for the Blue Lagoon, this prominent geothermal area – named a Unesco Global Geopark in 2015 – has countless *other* unique geological landscapes. A hub for spelunkers, geothermal hot springs and bird cliffs, it's now also home to brand new earth as a live volcano erupts.

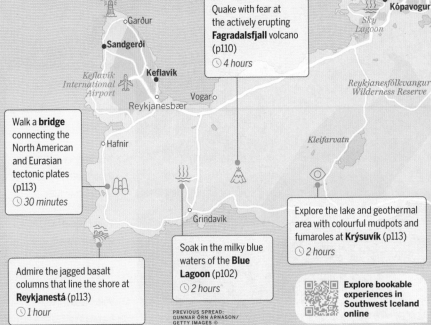

Quake with fear at the actively erupting **Fagradalsfjall** volcano (p110)
🕐 4 hours

Walk a **bridge** connecting the North American and Eurasian tectonic plates (p113)
🕐 30 minutes

Admire the jagged basalt columns that line the shore at **Reykjanestá** (p113)
🕐 1 hour

Soak in the milky blue waters of the **Blue Lagoon** (p102)
🕐 2 hours

Explore the lake and geothermal area with colourful mudpots and fumaroles at **Krýsuvík** (p113)
🕐 2 hours

Explore bookable experiences in Southwest Iceland online

PREVIOUS SPREAD:
GUNNAR ÖRN ÁRNASON/
GETTY IMAGES ©

Practicalities

ARRIVING

Keflavík International Airport
On the Reykjanes Peninsula, 50km from Reykjavík. The drive to and from Reykjavík is short and the roads are good. Buses depart regularly between Keflavík and Reykjavík.

FIND YOUR WAY

A tourist information centre can be found at the Duus Museum in Reykjanesbær.

MONEY

Volcano visitors can park in a paid lot (1000kr). Credit or debit cards are widely accepted around the peninsula.

WHERE TO STAY

Town	Pro/Con
Reykjanesbær	Close to the airport, with cultural museums and restaurants.
Grindavík	Charming fishing village, but with limited food and lodging options.
Suðurnesjabær	Quiet coastal villages with few tourists; limited eating options.

EATING & DRINKING

Fish and chips An active fishing industry provides tasty freshly caught fish for places like Issi food truck in Njarðvík.

Beer Sample a local brew on tap at Litla Brugghúsið in Suðurnesjabær.

Must-try fish soup Cafe Bryggjan (p113)

Best spot for a drink Cafe Petite (p113)

GETTING AROUND

Car Driving is the best way to explore places off the beaten path.

Tour Bus tours for those who want to sit back and take it all in.

Bus Strætó (straeto.is) buses service Keflavík Airport and the Blue Lagoon.

APR–MAY
Cooler temperatures, brown landscapes.

JUN–AUG
Everything is green, fair temperatures, midnight sun.

SEP–OCT
Rain and wind is very common.

NOV–MAR
Snowy with limited daylight hours.

SOUTHWEST ICELAND & REYKJANES PENINSULA FIND YOUR FEET

09 Soak in the Blue LAGOON

OTHER-WORLDLY | HOT SPRING | REJUVENATING

When you think of Iceland, no doubt one of the first things that comes to mind is the Blue Lagoon. Walking out in a fluffy white bathrobe to milky-blue water surrounded by lava, is the epitome of relaxation and luxury. Conveniently located 20 minutes from the airport, there's a reason it's the most visited tourist destination on the island.

ALEKSANDAR TODOROVIC/SHUTTERSTOCK ©

SOUTHWEST ICELAND & REYKJANES PENINSULA EXPERIENCES

How to

When to go Early in the morning or after 6pm to avoid crowds. Reservation required for entry.

Getting here It's only 20 minutes from Keflavík International Airport and 40 minutes from Reykjavík. Destination Blue Lagoon and Reykjavík

Excursions both offer bus services. Taxis are available from Keflavík or Reykjavík.

Luggage Storage is available on-site.

Changing facilities Private lockers are included with entrance as are shampoo and conditioner in the showers.

SKYNESHER/GETTY IMAGES ©

WANDERLUSTER/GETTY IMAGES ©

Admission to the Blue Lagoon includes the following perks:

Lagoon Relax and soak in the milky-blue waters, which are full of minerals, algae and silica. Kept at a piping 38°C, it doesn't matter if it's cold or snowy outside, the water will keep you warm. Most people spend about two hours here.

Mask bar Apply an algae or silica mud mask to your face and arms for a fresh glow. Algae contains collagen, so it helps reduce fine lines and wrinkles. Silica is cleansing and brightens the skin. The perfect jet lag cure.

Steam room and sauna Take a break from the lagoon and hop into the dry or moist heat. Nourishing for the whole body.

Swim-up bar Refresh with a selection of juices, smoothies, beer and wine. Your electronic bracelet keeps your tab, so you can pay as you leave.

Viewing deck Grab your robe and head to the 2nd floor for a great view over the lagoon.

Tips for Your Visit

First, follow pool etiquette (p104). Second, load up on conditioner, as the minerals in the water are tough on hair. Third, leave all jewellery in the lockers to avoid damage. Fourth, bring your own swimsuit, robe or slippers, or rent them at the counter; also bring a waterproof case for your phone – it'll be handy if you want to take it with you into the lagoon. Finally, don't just hang out by the entrance and the mask bar. The lagoon is large and quiet corners can be found if you explore.

Clockwise from bottom left
A bather relaxes; The Blue Lagoon; Swim-up bar

 Indulge Yourself

Upgrade your Blue Lagoon experience with a premium add-on:

Massage Treat your muscles to a massage while suspended in the water.

Retreat Spa The ultimate five-hour luxury spa experience, including body scrubs and private facilities.

Dining Experience fine dining at the Moss or Lava Restaurant or grab a bite at the Spa Restaurant or cafe.

Accommodation Stay overnight at the Silica or Retreat Hotel.

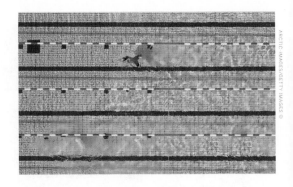

Pool Etiquette

GUIDELINES TO ENJOY ICELAND'S MOST LOVED TRADITION

Icelanders love swimming pools. Almost every town has one. Baby swim classes are offered starting from four months old. Families spend weekends soaking in hot water and splashing down slides. However, in order to enjoy the pools, there are rules you must follow.

Left A swimmer does laps **Middle** Seljavallalaug hot spring pool **Right** Outdoor geothermally heated shower

Admission

Stop at the entry counter and pay the admission fee. Entrance is 700kr to 1000kr for adults, 100kr to 200kr for kids, and free for babies and the elderly. If you don't have a swimsuit, you can rent one.

Shoes Off

There are separate changing rooms for men and women. Children can use either changing facility under parental supervision. Before entering the changing room, take off your shoes. There is a rack outside both men's and women's changing rooms where everyone leaves their shoes.

Changing Rooms

Inside the changing rooms you will find lockers. They are free to use and have a key attached to safely store your belongings. Leave your phone and camera as they are forbidden inside the locker room and there's nowhere to put them once outside. Get undressed, grab your suit and towel, and head to the showers. There will be cubbies to store your towel until you are finished.

Wash First

The most important rule is to wash your entire body without a bathing suit on. Soap is provided, but you are welcome to bring your own. There is a poster in every shower detailing the areas that need to be washed with soap before entering the pool. The pools use minimal chlorine, so this is important to keep everything sanitary. Some pools have a stall with a shower curtain if you want more privacy.

Entering the Pools

After showering, put your bathing suit on and head to the pool. Leave your towel in the cubbies so that it's ready when you come back inside. In the pool area you will find hot-pots of varying temperatures as well as a lap pool and possibly a slide or splash area for kids. Hop around to as many hot-pots as you like, and take a dip in the cold pool to cool off in between. Some pools are indoors, others are outdoors, or some have a combination.

> You will find hot-pots of varying temperatures as well as a lap pool and possibly a slide or splash area for kids.

Time to Go

When you are finished enjoying your time, go back and do everything in reverse. Shower, dry yourself off completely (do not enter the changing area with wet feet!), find your locker and get dressed, and put your shoes on outside as you leave.

Congratulations! You have now experienced one of the essential parts of Icelandic culture, and you did so while following the best tourist etiquette. Go forth and have a great day now that you are in a state of bliss.

🍨 Post-Swim Treat

After your relaxing session at the pool, do as the Icelanders do and head to an ice-cream shop. For the local experience get the Bragðarefur, which is soft-serve ice cream blended together with your choice of fruits or candies. Go-to places include Ísbúð Huppu or Ísbúð Vesturbæjar, or if you prefer hand-scooped ice cream look for Skubb or Valdis.

10 Not the Blue
LAGOON

LOCAL | POOL | REFRESHING

In Iceland, going to the pools is a way of life. Every day locals gather in hot tubs heated with geothermal water. They're more than a place to swim; they're a place to discuss the news, gossip about neighbours and soak away stress. It's part of the daily routine, and no matter the weather – under the midnight sun or during a snowstorm in the dark days of winter – you will find the pools packed.

© 2021 CHRISTOPHER LUND

🗺 How to

Getting here Rent a car to choose your own hot-pool adventure.

When to go Year-round, rain or shine.

Expect to pay 8000kr for Sky Lagoon; 1000kr for local pools.

What to bring Swimsuit, towel, toiletries.

SKY LAGOON/PURSUIT ©

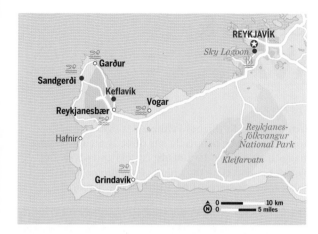

Top The Sky Lagoon **Bottom** Sky Lagoon guest

Sky Lagoon

'Where the sea meets the sky' is the motto of this brand-new spa experience. The architecture is inspired by Icelandic design elements using turf, water and lava. The infinity pool overlooks the Atlantic with views all the way to the Snæfellsnes Peninsula. A swim-up bar serves a selection of non-alcoholic and alcoholic drinks. It's the ultimate place for relaxation and rejuvenation, just minutes from downtown Reykjavík.

The complete Sky Lagoon experience is based on a series of thoughtful, curated steps designed to help you relax from head to toe:

Hot dip Wade in the hot waters of the lagoon, get a natural massage under the waterfall, or rest on the lava rocks.

Cold dip Plunge into the cold pool to get your blood pumping.

Sweat it out Step into the sauna for quiet serenity and sweat it out with an incredible view.

Refresh Walk through a cold mist to refresh your senses.

Exfoliate Massage with their signature body scrub, a mix of sea salt and oils.

Steam Step into a hot steam room and allow the scrub to melt in and hydrate your skin.

Relax Shower and hop back in the lagoon.

If you worked up an appetite, the lounge inside serves a selection of quick bites and beverages. Reservations to the lagoon complex are recommended.

Take a Dip

If you're looking to experience Icelandic pool culture without the spa price tag, a town's local *sundlaug* is your best bet. Make sure you check opening times in advance. The following villages have pools worth exploring:

Reykjanesbær
Four hot tubs, steam bath, indoor and outdoor lap pool, children's pool.

Vogar
Hot tub, lap pool, solarium.

Garður
Two hot tubs, sauna, lap pool, children's pool, waterslide.

Sandgerði
Two hot tubs, sauna, lap pool, children's pool, two waterslides.

Grindavík
Two hot tubs, cold tub, sauna, lap pool, children's pool, waterslide.

11 Eruptions & **LAVA**

VOLCANOES | LAVA FIELDS | CAVES

▬▬▬ The geological landscape on the Reykjanes Peninsula is evidence of hundreds of years of volcanic activity. The peninsula sits directly on a diverging fault line in which earthquakes have created lava fields, craters and caves. But you don't have to be a geologist to appreciate the unique formations: a drive around the peninsula reveals captivating areas just waiting to be explored.

MT UEHRING/GETTY IMAGES ©

🗺 How to

Getting here Rent a car to explore off-the-beaten-path places, or join a tour.

When to go Guided cave tours take place year-round, but hikes and off-trail exploration shouldn't be attempted between November and March due to dangerous snow and wind conditions.

Expect to pay 7000kr to 44,000kr for cave tours.

What to wear Warm layers and waterproof clothing from head to toe no matter what time of year. Sturdy hiking boots are a must for the rugged volcanic terrain.

SOFYA DUSKHINA/SHUTTERSTOCK ©

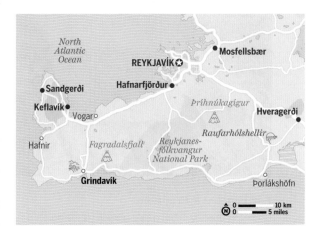

Top Fagradalsfjall **Bottom** Flowing lava, Fagradalsfjall

Hike to an Erupting Volcano

What better way to experience the power of an erupting volcano than by witnessing hot flowing lava in person? Fagradalsfjall volcano allows visitors to do just that. Locals and tourists alike have been hiking to the eruption site since it began in March 2021. A trail has been carved out so that people can walk to the volcano and enjoy this once-in-a-lifetime experience from a safe distance. Note: daylight hours vary according to time of year. In June, when the sun essentially never sets, you could be at the eruption site at 2am and feel like it's the middle of the day. By contrast, the sun sets around 10pm in August, meaning it's possible to view the red-hot lava in complete darkness.

Paid parking lots, off Rte 427, are just east of the village Grindavík. Expect the hike to last three to four hours round-trip, depending on your pace. Sturdy hiking boots are essential, as are warm layers and waterproof gear. Consider hiking poles and headlamps too, and bring a backpack with water and a snack. Volunteer emergency responders are on-site for a few hours per day. Due to gasses that the volcano emits, the hiking route is closed some days. Check online (safetravel.is) for the latest info on the hiking route, GPS coordinates and weather conditions.

Ongoing lava flow means hiking paths may be periodically blocked. It's possible to sidestep such problems by observing Fagradalsfjall from the air. Helicopter operators, such as Heli Austria (heliaustriaiceland.is; 50,000kr per person), may also be able to land near the volcano, allowing for photos.

⛰ Explore Lava Tubes

Lava tubes are formed when lava hardens over a flowing magma channel. On the Reykjanes Peninsula there are two prominent tubes that can be explored with a guided tour.

Raufarhólshellir

Walk through the path that lava flowed during the Leitahraun eruption about 5200 years ago. Natural holes in the ceiling reveal multicoloured rocks as you walk through the lava tube. (thelavatunnel.is)

Þríhnúkagígur

Descend via elevator into a 200m dormant volcano that could house the Statue of Liberty! Expert guides ensure safety during the slow six-minute descent as you marvel at the walls where magma once flowed. (insidethevolcano.com)

NATHAN MORTIMER/SHUTTERSTOCK ©

■ With thanks to Sara Barsotti

Sara works for Veður as a volcanic hazards coordinator.

Volcanoes

HOW THE ISLAND WAS FORMED

Iceland sits atop a hotspot on the divergent Mid-Atlantic Ridge. This results in frequent volcanic activity and landscapes filled with lava fields, black-sand beaches, peaks and craters. The island has about 30 active volcanic systems, one of which is currently erupting.

Left Bárðarbunga's volcanic crater
Middle Grímsvötn ash plume **Right** Magma flows from Fagradalsfjall

Earthquakes & Eruptions

Iceland formed 20 million years ago when the plate boundaries of the Mid-Atlantic Ridge spread apart, releasing magma from the centre of the earth, creating what we now call Iceland. Iceland is still in the making to this day with current eruptions and lava flow creating new earth.

Because of its plate-boundary location, earthquakes are common. Around 500 are recorded in an average week. Most of these are mere tremors less than magnitude 3 and not felt by humans. Occasionally a magnitude 4 or 5 will hit an active volcanic zone, which can be felt around the area. Because the plates are diverging, a magnitude 5.0 and above is significant. Bigger earthquakes are rare; the largest recorded was a magnitude 7.1 in 1784.

Iceland is among the most active volcanic areas on Earth, with about 30 active systems. On average eruptions occur every five to 10 years. Since Iceland's settlement, 13 systems have erupted. Most were from fissures or shield volcanoes that produce basaltic lava. The dangers of volcanic eruptions include hot lava flow, poisonous gases, ash fall, lightning and glacial flooding. Depending on the location and type of volcano, any combination of these hazards is possible. Eruptions can happen at any time, but are usually preceded by an earthquake.

On 19 March 2021, after a three-week period of seismic activity, a fissure opened on the Reykjanes Peninsula. Over the next weeks, several vents opened and increasing lava flow filled up Geldingadalur valley and spilled over into neighbouring valleys. Less than two months after the onset, one massive crater took over, spraying magma up

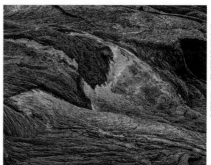

to 300m into the air like a geyser. The fissure, aka Fagradals-fjall volcano, is a subset of the Krýsuvík volcanic system, one of four systems on the Reykjanes Peninsula. The last eruption happened over 800 years ago, but the entire peninsula was re-activated in December 2019 with small, frequent earthquakes. In February, elevated seismicity preceded the eruption, including 60 earthquakes above magnitude 4 and seven above magnitude 5. On 24 February, a magnitude 5.7 earthquake shook the peninsula. Three weeks later, a dyke intrusion finally found a weakness in the crust at Fagradalsfjall.

> Iceland is among the most active volcanic areas on Earth, with about 30 active systems.

The effusive eruption continues with magma pouring out and forming cones in the lava field. If this continues long enough, it will create a shield volcano, which means it was created or shaped by the lava flow itself. This eruption has been increasing since the onset. Current dangers to the public are gas emissions and the spread of hot lava.

A Way of Life

Despite their dangers, Icelanders have come to rely on volcanic systems. Geothermal energy brings hot water directly to homes and allows greenhouses to grow fresh fruits and vegetables year-round. The country is a major advocate of renewable energy, producing 30% of its electricity from geothermal stations. Swimming pools, part of Iceland's social fabric, are naturally heated with this hot water, and the tourism industry utilises volcanoes for tours and excursions.

🌋 Other Recent Eruptions

Eldfell Heimaey, the inhabited island of the Vestmannaeyjar archipelago, erupted without warning in January 1973. Residents had to evacuate on fishing boats and the lava flow caused massive destruction in the town.

Eyjafjallajökull Located under the glacier in South Iceland. Ash from its April 2010 eruption disrupted airspace for days, affecting millions of travellers.

Grímsvötn Iceland's most active volcano, situated under the Vatnajökull glacier in the central highlands, erupted in May 2011, sending a massive ash cloud into the sky.

Bárðarbunga The largest eruption in over 200 years lasted from August 2014 to February 2015. Locals were concerned with gas pollution and glacial flooding.

Listings

BEST OF THE REST

Lighthouses & Views

Garður

At the northernmost tip of the peninsula is a small village with two lighthouses. It's a beautiful area to explore the coastline and spot birds or seals. Stop by the nearby heritage museum, which has a collection of old machine engines, or visit the exhibitions inside the larger of the two lighthouses.

Reykjanesviti

Located on the southwestern part of the peninsula near Reykjanestá and Gunnuhver hot springs. It was originally built in 1878, but an earthquake destroyed it a few years later. It was rebuilt in 1929 made of white concrete in a new location. Walk up to the lighthouse for a great view over the area.

Stafnesviti

A picturesque orange lighthouse sits between Hafnir and Sandgerði. Large waves can usually be seen crashing around the shore of the surrounding dramatic landscape. The farm nearby was once the most prominent fishing area on the peninsula in the 17th and 18th centuries.

Hópsnesviti

Just south of the village of Grindavík sits a small orange lighthouse. Accessible by car or foot, the route to the lighthouse runs through a lava field dotted with remnants of old rusted shipwrecks.

History & Culture

The Icelandic Museum of Rock 'n' Roll

Experience the history of popular music in Iceland with an iPad guided tour of this Reykjanesbær museum. Channel your inner musician by trying out different instruments in the sound lab and record a video of yourself doing karaoke.

Viking World

Also in Reykjanesbær, this museum showcases the settlement of Iceland and the Nordic role in discovering North America. The main hall features the *Íslendingur*, an exact replica of a 9th-century Viking ship that sailed from Iceland to New York to commemorate Leifur Eiríksson's journey to the New World.

Stekkjarkot

Next to Viking World is a turf-house replica of how Icelandic families once lived. Open to the public with free admission.

Duus Museum

Houses multiple art and cultural exhibits in the charming harbour of Keflavík. Also a tourist centre for information about the surrounding area.

Giantess in a Cave

A nod to the troll and elves folklore that exists in Iceland. Visit a 5m-tall giant sitting in a cave

GLASSHOUSE IMAGES/GETTY IMAGES © ARCHITECT: GUÐMUNDUR JÓNSSON

Viking World

in Reykjanesbær. It has a mailbox for children to leave letters and a tree where babies leave their pacifiers. Climb onto the giant's lap for a photo op.

Interesting Geological Features

Reykjanestá & Gunnuhver

Jagged basalt columns, a lighthouse, and a geothermal area with colourful mudpots and fumaroles.

Bridge Between Continents

A built bridge connecting the North American and Eurasian tectonic plates.

Brimketill

A seaside pool naturally carved by the ocean. Legend has it the trolls used to bathe in it.

Krýsuvík

Lake Kleifarvatn and Seltun make up this geothermal area with colourful mudpots and fumaroles.

Grænavatn

A 6000-year-old crater lake with green water. Located north of Seltún and easy to walk around.

Stampar

This series of calderas is around 2000 years old. It's a short walk from the marked parking lot just off Rte 425.

Stóra-Eldborg

The biggest of five calderas and 7000 years old. From Rte 427 it's possible to walk up to the crater or simply view it from afar.

Háleyjarbunga

A 9000-year-old 25m-deep caldera near Reykjanestá. It can be reached from a hiking path that starts from Gunnuhver.

Stafnesviti

Coffee & Cakes

Cafe Petite

Sink into comfortable living-room furniture-with your beverage of choice at this Reykjanesbær cafe. Pour your own beer on tap right at your table, or order your favourite coffee drink.

Cafe Bryggjan

A cosy fishing-themed cafe in the Grindavík harbour. Locals and tourists alike gather around the few tables for a cup of joe or a selection of homemade cakes and Icelandic waffles. If you're in the mood for something savoury, try the mouth-watering seafood soup with fresh baked bread.

Hjá Höllu

The place to go in Grindavík if you're looking for fresh healthy food. Serving smoothies, sandwiches and salads made with minimal ingredients.

Scan to find more things to do in Southwest Iceland online

12 Vestmannaeyjar
SIDE TRIP

PUFFINS | WHALES | VOLCANOES

The archipelago of 15 dome-shaped islands, collectively known as Vestmannaeyjar, sits on a volcanic hotspot just 16km off the southern coast. The largest island, Heimaey, is inhabited by a community referred to as the Eyjamenn – the island people – by 'continental' Icelanders.

How to

Getting there The ferry to Heimaey (herjolfur.is) departs from Landeyjahöfn (35 minutes) in summer and Þorlákshöfn (three hours) in winter; winter visitors should overnight on the island. Reykjavík Domestic Airport has several flights a week.

Festival At the end of July, 10,000 to 15,000 Icelanders flock to Vestmannaeyjar for the four-day Þjóðhátíð pop-music festival.

Dining Some visitors travel to the island just to dine at internationally praised Slippurinn restaurant.

Map:
- 0 — 1 km
- 0 — 0.5 miles
- North Atlantic Ocean
- Ystiklettur
- Heimaklettur
- Klettsvik
- Blátindur
- Vestmannaeyjar
- Heimaey
- Eldheimar Museum
- Eldfell
- Helgafell
- Sæfjall
- Stórhöfði

The Backyard Volcano

In casual geological terms, the town of Vestmannaeyjar is the 'Pompeii of the North': in 1973, the town had to be rebuilt after a volcanic eruption forced the population to flee on a cold January night.

The eruption lasted six months and the **Eldfell** crater looming over the town is easily recognisable by its cone shape and lack of vegetation. By foot it takes an hour from town, but if your legs are tired, quad company Volcano ATV (volcanoatv.is) can get you there.

Preserving the history of this major event in Iceland's history, is the **Eldheimar Museum** with an immersive exhibition and an excellent sideshow on the 1963 Surtsey eruption.

Top right Puffins on Vestmannaeyjar **Bottom right** View of Heimaey

VENTURA/SHUTTERSTOCK ©

🦆 Biggest Love Island: for Puffins

The Vestmannaeyjar archipelago is home to the world's largest Atlantic puffin colony. Every summer, starting in June, these 'penguins of the North' arrive at their seaside burrows at cape Stórhöfði, Heimaklettur and elsewhere to do a little dance, make a little love. Tours available.

Little Gray & Little White

In 2019 a pair of **beluga whales** that previously lived at an aquarium in China came, via plane, to Vestmannaeyjar for show-biz retirement. Their new home is a 32,000-sq-metre sea pen at a pristine creek called Klettsvik – accessible by excursion boat (adult/child 7500/5000kr) – where one of the caretakers explains the mission of this sanctuary for cetaceans. The Sea Life Trust (belugasanctuary. sealifetrust.org) hosting the belugas also has a **visitor centre** explaining the island's marine life and the 6000-mile journey made by the two seasoned performers, Little Gray and Little White.

SOUTH COAST & SOUTHERN HIGHLANDS

WATERFALLS | GLACIERS | BLACK-SAND BEACHES

**Experience
South Coast
online**

SOUTH COAST
Trip Builder

Hike the painted mountains of **Landmannalaugar** (p126)
⏱ 1 day

Explore bookable experiences in the South Coast online

Brennisteinsalda

△ *Bláhnúkur*

△ *Fjallabak Nature Reserve*

▬▬▬ Follow the coastal route for the standard sights, but don't be afraid to head inland to explore less-travelled parts. Þjórsárdalur valley and the highland areas of Þórsmörk and Landmannalaugar will get you away from the crowds and into some incredible nature.

Walk behind the stunning cascade at **Seljalandsfoss** (p121)
⏱ 1 hour

Fljótsdalur

Þrongá

Head into the highlands for some hiking in **Þórsmörk** (p124)
⏱ 1 day

Markarfljót

○ Stóra-Dímon

△ *Tindfjöll*

Valahnúkur

Hvolsvöllur (9km);
Selfoss (57km);
Hvergerði (70km)

○ Stóra-Mörk III

Eyjafjallajökull

Fimmvörðuháls

Mýrdalsjökull

Skógaheiði

Sólheimajökull

Stroll on the black-sand beach and admire the basalt stacks at **Reynisfjara** (p123)
⏱ 1 hour

Gape at **Skógafoss** from the ground or above (p121)
⏱ 1 hour

○ Ásólfsskáli

Skógar

North Atlantic Ocean

Admire the rock formations at **Dyrhólaey** (p123)
⏱ 1 hour

Brekkur ○

Vík ○

Ⓝ 0 ——— 20 km
0 ——— 10 miles

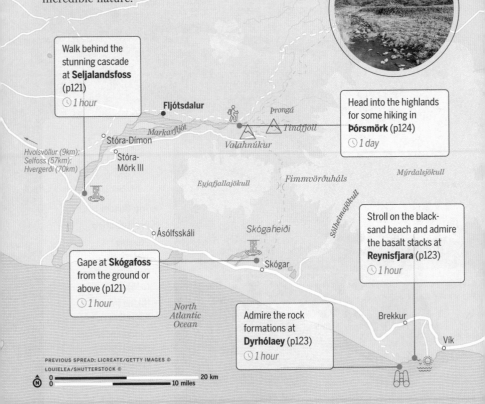

Practicalities

ARRIVING

Keflavík International Airport Located 165km from Seljalandsfoss. The roads from Reykjavík are good and buses run frequently.

FIND YOUR WAY

Tourist information centres can be found at Hveragerði, Selfoss and Vík.

MONEY

Expect to pay for parking at Seljalandsfoss and for public toilets at Dyrhólaey. Credit or debit cards are widely accepted.

WHERE TO STAY

Town	Pro/Con
Selfoss	Major hub with restaurants and accommodation; good location from which to tackle South Coast sights.
Hvolsvöllur	Small village with few amenities situated close to major landmarks.
Vík	Biggest town in the South but also the busiest and most expensive.

EATING & DRINKING

Dine in a barn Gamla Fjósið (p128)

Fresh fish and chips Mia's Country Wagon (p128)

Local beer Craft brewery Smiðjan Brugghús (pictured) in Vík offers brews on tap.

Best for viking-themed dining Ingólfsskáli (p128)

Must-try cheese pizza Suður-Vík (p128)

GETTING AROUND

Car Driving is the best way to explore places off the beaten path.

Tour A bus tour is a good option for those who want to sit back and take it all in.

Bus Strætó buses stop at the villages along the coast. (straeto.is)

APR–MAY
Cooler temperatures, brown landscapes.

JUN–AUG
Everything is green, fair temperatures, midnight sun.

SEP–OCT
Rain and wind is very common.

NOV–MAR
Snowy with limited daylight hours.

13 Chasing
WATERFALLS

NATURE | HIKES | VIEWS

Iceland has thousands of waterfalls, but some of the most popular and impressive are located on the South Coast. Thanks to run-off from the glaciers, you can find yourself at the base of massive waterfalls within two hours of leaving Reykjavík. Each fall is unique in its size, shape, volume and surrounding nature, and all of them are worth a visit.

VADYM LAVRA/SHUTTERSTOCK ©

🗺 How to

Getting here Rent a car to visit hidden gems and stay as long as you like. Guided tours stop at the main waterfalls as part of any South Coast trip.

When to go These major attractions are always busy, but tour buses arrive between 10am and 4pm, making them extra-crowded.

Paid parking It's 700kr to park at Seljalandsfoss.

What to wear Waterproof gear from head to toe. Microspikes are needed to avoid slips on icy paths between November and March.

DANIEL.FREYR/SHUTTERSTOCK ©

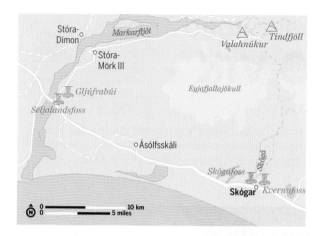

Seljalandsfoss You'll see this waterfall from afar as you're driving east on the Ring Rd. It's a 60m drop-off from a sheer cliff, but what makes it unique is that you can walk behind the falls. Make sure you have waterproof outerwear because you will get wet, and sturdy boots are essential as the waterfall mist makes for a slippery pathway. From November to March a thick layer of ice forms on the path making it impassable without microspikes. Afterwards, head to the food truck for refreshments and take in the view from a distance.

Skógafoss Sits in the village of Skógar where a handful of lucky locals have a massive waterfall in their backyard. A wide curtain of water falls 60m surrounded by lush vegetation. It's possible to approach the falls to feel the power up close, but be prepared to get wet. Don't forget to take the nearly 500 stairs to the top platform for sweeping views over the valley. This is also the start of the Fimmvörðuháls hike, a 25km trail that ends in Þórsmörk (p124).

Gljúfrabúi Just 500m from Seljalandsfoss and tucked behind a rock wall, this gem falls 40m down into a cave. To get inside, you walk through a river with slippery rocks by holding onto the cave wall. Once inside you're rewarded with thunderous falls.

Kvernufoss Behind the Skogar folk museum tucked back into a ravine is a surprising gem. A 30m drop from a cliff surrounded by black rock makes this remote location a must-see. To get there, head behind the museum and follow the river for about 20 minutes.

Top Seljalandsfoss **Bottom** Kvernufoss

🏔 Stunning Waterfalls

Glaciers cover 11% of the land in Iceland. Waterfalls on the South Coast are fed from Eyjafjallajökull and Mýrdalsjökull glaciers. Melting of these ice caps means water finds its way to the sea through cracks and over cliffs. The result is stunning waterfalls in various locations and landscapes.

14 Coast Road Trip
TO VÍK

SCENIC | COASTAL | WATERFALLS

Massive waterfalls, sweeping black-sand beaches and glaciers that cascade down the mountainside are just a few things you will see between Reykjavík and Vík. Packed with breathtaking sights, this South Coast drive is a must-do during your time in Iceland.

CANYALCIN/
SHUTTERSTOCK ©

🗺 Trip Notes

Getting here Rent a car or join a guided tour.

When to go Peak season is June to September. Difficult driving conditions could slow you down between November and March.

Top tip Route 1 is a two-lane road with no shoulder, so stopping on the side of the road is dangerous. Find a rest area if you want to pull over for a photo op.

🚶 Worthwhile Detours

Detour off the main road to these wonderfully scenic places:

Þórsmörk Part of the highlands with hiking galore. Reached via 4WD or guided tour due to difficult roads and river crossings.

Vestmannaeyjar Take the ferry to an archipelago of volcanic islands. A village occupies Heimaey island, home to a recent eruption and great puffin watching May to August.

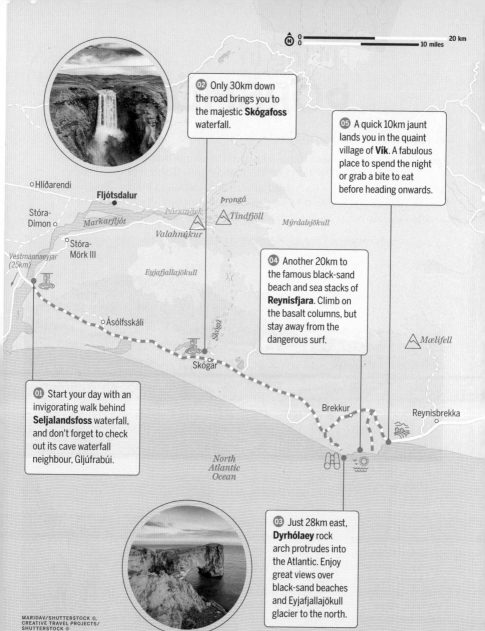

02 Only 30km down the road brings you to the majestic **Skógafoss** waterfall.

05 A quick 10km jaunt lands you in the quaint village of **Vík**. A fabulous place to spend the night or grab a bite to eat before heading onwards.

04 Another 20km to the famous black-sand beach and sea stacks of **Reynisfjara**. Climb on the basalt columns, but stay away from the dangerous surf.

01 Start your day with an invigorating walk behind **Seljalandsfoss** waterfall, and don't forget to check out its cave waterfall neighbour, Gljúfrabúi.

03 Just 28km east, **Dyrhólaey** rock arch protrudes into the Atlantic. Enjoy great views over black-sand beaches and Eyjafjallajökull glacier to the north.

Hlíðarendi

Fljótsdalur

Stóra-Dímon

Markarfljót

Þórsmörk

ÞronGá

Tindfjöll

Mýrdalsjökull

Valahnúkur

Stóra-Mörk III

Vestmannaeyjar (25km)

Eyjafjallajökull

Ásólfsskáli

Skógá

Mælifell

Skógar

Brekkur

Reynisbrekka

North Atlantic Ocean

20 km

10 miles

15 Hiking in ÞÓRSMÖRK

OUTDOORS | HIGHLANDS | NATURE

Þórsmörk is located in the southern highlands between three glaciers: Eyjafjallajökull, Mýrdalsjökull and Tindfjallajökull. It translates to 'Thor's Valley' and is known for its rugged nature and unlimited hiking. This protected nature reserve is teeming with jagged green mountains, deep ravines and braided glacier rivers ideal for outdoor enthusiasts and photographers alike.

LUIGIMORBIDELLI/GETTY IMAGES ©

🗺 How to

Getting here River crossings mean a 4WD will only get so far; hop on one of the modified buses to complete the journey. In summer Trex, Sterna and Reykjavík Excursions run from Reykjavík. Hire a super-Jeep tour with Midgard Adventure to get you there and show you all the gems.

When to go Year-round with a tour. June to September if you're driving.

Top tip Bring food, as base camps have cooking facilities, or visit LavaGrill restaurant at Volcano Huts.

HENN PHOTOGRAPHY/GETTY IMAGES ©

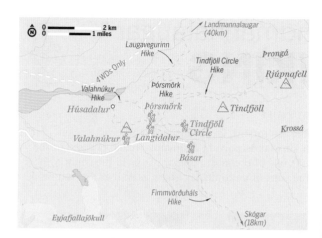

Top View over Fimmvörðuháls trailhead **Bottom** Hikers along Fimmvörðuháls Pass

Hikes around Þórsmörk range from two hours to multiple days. Trail maps can be found at the base camps.

Valahnúkur This moderately difficult 2.4km hike starts at Volcano Huts in Husadalur and gives panoramic views over the entire valley. From the summit you can see two glaciers, braided glacial rivers and endless moss-covered mountains.

Tindfjöll Circle A longer loop that traverses some gorgeous nature. Trail markers begin at Langidalur, but it can also be reached from Volcano Huts. Parts of the trail are narrow with steep drop-offs. Sweeping valley views reward you along the way. Expect the 8km hike to take between five and six hours.

Multi-day hikes The Laugavegur and Fimmvörðuháls trails start/end in Þórsmörk. Basar marks the beginning of Fimmvörðuháls, and Laugavegur ends at Langidalur. These hikes shouldn't be attempted without proper gear and planning.

Fimmvörðuháls

This 25km trail runs between Skógafoss and Þórsmörk. The hike is broken up into three sections. Part 1 is Waterfall Way, a series of 26 waterfalls from the Skogá river. Part 2 passes between the two glaciers: Eyjafjallajökull and Mýrdalsjökull. Part 3 is in the lush green mountains of Þórsmörk. This hike requires appropriate gear, planning and preparation. Weather conditions are unpredictable, so warm layers, waterproof outerwear and sturdy hiking boots are essential. Bring plenty of food and water. Most hikers complete the trail within eight to 10 hours, but you can overnight at a mountain hut halfway.

🛏 Stay Overnight

The following base camps are generally open June to September. You need to reserve for hut accommodation but not for camping. Þórsmörk is a nature reserve, so camping outside designated areas is forbidden.

Basar Huts for 83 persons, kitchen and outdoor sitting area, showers for a fee and a campground. (utivist.is)

Husadalur Private cottages, shared dormitories, glamping tents and a campground. Kitchen, sitting area and showers. Restaurant serves three hot meals daily. (volcanotrails.com)

Langidalur Hut for 75 persons, a fully equipped kitchen, showers for a fee and a campground. (fi.is)

Slyppugil Camping area with toilets and shower for a fee, but no kitchen or electricity. (tjalda.is)

16 Landmannalaugar
HIKING

HIGHLANDS | CAMPING | ACTIVITIES

Multicoloured rhyolite mountains, lava fields and geothermal steam vents make up the breathtaking landscape of Landmannalaugar. Located in the Fjallabak Nature Reserve, it's one of the most popular places in the country for hiking. The base camp is the start of multiple day hikes, as well as the famous 55km Laugavegurinn trek.

LOUIELEA/SHUTTERSTOCK ©

How to

Getting here Drive a 4WD on one of three routes: F208 from the north, and F225 or F208 from the south. Trex and Reykjavík Excursions have daily bus departures from Reykjavík.

When to go June to September when the highland roads open, depending on weather.

Top tip Mountain Mall is an old-school bus from the '70s that sells snacks and basic supplies. Otherwise, bring your own food.

Sleeping Camping and hut accommodation available with kitchen and showers at the base camp.

PYTY/SHUTTERSTOCK ©

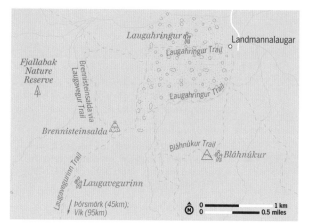

Top Landmannalaugar landscape
Bottom Hikers ascend the path at Landmannalaugar

Popular Hikes

There are countless hikes of varying duration and difficulty around Landmannalaugar. Check at the base camp for maps of hiking trails around the area. The most popular routes are Laugahringur, Brennisteinsalda and Bláhnúkur.

Laugahringur A 5km loop through a lava field. Relatively easy walking, this path would be great for kids or families.

Brennisteinsalda An old volcano and an iconic mountain in Landmannalaugar known for its vibrant colours. The beginning of the hike is the same as Laugahringur before continuing upwards to the mountain peak. This 6km loop offers great highland views.

Bláhnúkur A more challenging route, but the one with the ● most rewarding views. A 6km loop with steep narrow paths has fantastic panoramic views at the summit. If you have time, it's possible to combine the Bláhnúkur and Brennisteinsalda hikes.

Laugavegurinn This 55km trek runs from Landmannalaugar to Þórsmörk, traversing some of Iceland's most incredible scenery. It's only accessible between July and September and is usually completed in three to five days with stops at mountain huts along the way. To reserve a bed or find camping info, check online (fi.is). Due to unpredictable highland weather, it's essential to have warm layers, waterproof outerwear and sturdy hiking boots. Hikers carry their own food with plenty of water reserves to fill up from the glacier streams along the way.

♨ Non-Hikers

Hiking isn't the only way to enjoy the beauty of Landmannalaugar.

Hot Spring

Landmannalaugar translates to 'the people's pool' for good reason: a big natural hot springs is located here. Relaxing with a dip in hot water is the perfect way to enjoy the surrounding nature.

Horseback Riding

Let the Icelandic horse bring you to places that are difficult to reach on foot. Multi-day guided tours can be arranged for more experienced riders.

Angling

Volcanic lakes around the area are full of brown trout and Arctic char. With a license, you can fish with your own pole, or join a tour where operators outfit you with everything you need.

Listings

BEST OF THE REST

Eat & Be Merry

Ingólfsskáli   €€

A Viking-themed restaurant inside an old turf longhouse. Staff dress up in old Icelandic clothing and the food is made with local ingredients. If you want to feel like a true Viking, drink your beer out of a horn. Ten-minute drive from Selfoss.

Gamla Fjósið   €€

An old barn converted into a restaurant serving delicious food. A 40km drive southeast of Hvolsvöllur.

Mia's Country Wagon   €

Just before you reach Skógafoss you'll find a colourful food truck selling fish and chips with freshly caught fish from a nearby village.

Suður-Vík   €€

This Vík restaurant is located inside an old aluminium home. Try the cheese pizza, which is made with four cheeses and served with jam – much better than it sounds!

Museums

Bobby Fischer Center

In 1972, American chess player Robert James Fischer became the world chess champion at a tournament in Reykjavík. Years later he became an Icelandic citizen. The museum located in Selfoss houses memorabilia from his time in Iceland. It also stands as a meeting place for chess players and hosts chess tournaments.

Lava Centre

Hvolsvöllur is home to LAVA – an interactive exhibit about Iceland's volcanoes and earthquakes. Feel what it's like to experience an earthquake and watch volcanic eruptions in a HD movie. The site also serves as a tourist information centre for the area.

Skógar Museum

Open-air museum with turf houses as well as an indoor museum with artefacts from around the area. Short distance off the Ring Rd, 34km west of Vík.

Icelandic Lava Show

Experience red-hot lava flowing up close and personal in Vík at this interactive demonstration of a volcanic eruption.

Hot Water & Hikes

Reykjadalur

Just outside the town of Hveragerði and tucked away in the mountains is a hot spring river in which you can bathe. To get there, you must complete a moderately challenging 3km hike, but the views along the way and relaxing in a hot spring at the end makes it worth it.

Skógar Museum

Seljavallalaug

One of the oldest pools in the country, this was built in 1923 by a local farmer who wanted to teach people how to swim. It sits at the base of Eyjafjallajökull glacier and is fed by natural hot water from the ground. To get there, take an easy 1.8km walk from the parking lot.

 Tours

Glacier Hike

Sólheimajökull is a glacier tongue off Mýrdalsjökull and is a popular spot to walk on a glacier. Doing so should only be done with a professional guide, as the glaciers are unstable and dangerous. Multiple companies operate tours here.

Highlands

If you're not renting a 4WD, but want to get into Landmannalaugar or Þórsmörk, Midgard

Glacier hiking, Sólheimajökul

Adventure offers day and multi-day super-Jeep tours to get you to locations off the beaten path.

Zipline Vík

Zip between canyons as you experience the landscape from above.

SOUTH COAST & SOUTHERN HIGHLANDS REVIEWS

MATTHEW MICAH WRIGHT/SHUTTERSTOCK ©

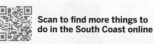

Scan to find more things to do in the South Coast online

THE EAST & SOUTHEAST

REMOTE FJORDS | VATNAJÖKULL NATIONAL PARK | SILENT PATHS

Experience
the East
online

THE EAST & SOUTHEAST
Trip Builder

The itinerary for Iceland's eastern corner is written in the colours of the Icelandic flag – blue, red and white – representing water, fire and ice. The sharp contrasts of the region will feed any traveller a balanced diet of excitement and calm energy: from the iconic glacial scenes at Jökulsárlón to the less-explored Eastfjords where economic success is still measured in fish.

Find solitude among the giant boulders of **Stórurð** (p153)
🕑 ½ day

Walk basalt cliffs in the newly discovered **Stuðlagil Canyon** (p148)
🕑 5 hours

Hug a tree in the sub-Arctic arboretum at **Hallormsstaður Forest** (p150)
🕑 ½ day

Enter Vatnajökull National Park on foot through the paths of **Skaftafell** (p134)
🕑 1 day

Browse restaurant menus in **Höfn**, arguably Iceland's seafood capital (p154)
🕑 ½ day

Sail past drifting icebergs at the **Jökulsárlón glacier lagoon** (p140)
🕑 3 hours

Hellisheiði eystri (20km)

Bakkagerði

Möðrudalur

Seyðisfjörður

Egilsstaðir

Mjóifjörður

Neskaupstaður

Lagarfljót

Hallormsstaður

Aðalból

Vattarnes

Fáskrúðsfjörður

Stöðvarfjörður

Breiðdalsvík

Hálslón Reservoir

Djúpivogur

Vatnajökull National Park

Höfn

Fagurhólsmýri

0   50 km
0   25 miles

Practicalities

ARRIVING

Seyðisfjörður Ferry Terminal To bring their own car, many travellers take the *Norræna* ferry (from Denmark).

Egilsstaðir & Höfn Airports Renting a car at the airports is the best option for onward travel.

FIND YOUR WAY

Vatnajökull National Park has visitor centres in Skaftafell and Skriðuklaustur. Visit visitegilsstadir. is and visitfjardabyggd.is.

MONEY

Cards are accepted everywhere. Expect to pay 11,000kr for a three-hour glacial hike and 2000kr for fish and chips.

WHERE TO STAY

Town	Pro/Con
Höfn	Wooden guesthouses and renovated warehouses line the busy, trawler-filled harbour.
Breiðdalsvík	One shop, one microbrewery, one public pool.
Egilsstaðir	The regional capital has a peculiar history of French architecture and an elegant waterfront hotel. Year-round lodging.

GETTING AROUND

Car Most practical way to travel. East of Höfn, the Ring Rd is less busy.

Bus Service is spotty. Try car-pooling website samferda.net.

Tunnels Several eastern villages are connected with mountain tunnels – the longest is 7km from Eskifjörður to Neskaupstaður.

EATING & DRINKING

Seafood Never tried halibut? Mackerel? Cusk? Browse the menus of this port region and learn new names of fish species.

Tea Vök Baths has a tea bar with colourful choices (p145).

Must-try restaurant Pakkhús (p155)

Best Ring Rd snack Fjalladýrð (p154)

NOV–MAR	**APR–MAY**	**JUN–AUG**	**SEP–OCT**
Ice-cave season and snowstorm warnings.	Low winter but too bright for Northern Lights.	Average temperatures around 15°C.	Spectacular streaks of colour and smaller crowds in Vatnajökull NP.

Exploring
SKAFTAFELL

GLACIER | WATERFALL | CAVES

Skaftafell is the gate to Vatnajökull National Park, a Unesco World Heritage Site, where guests walk into virgin birch-tree forests and then reach for a jacket as temperatures drop, the closer they get to the massive Vatnajökull glacier.

📍 How to

Getting there Drive to most sights via the Ring Rd; additional walking sometimes required. At Skaftafell visitors pay a parking fee (750kr per car), then walk 2.5km to Svartifoss waterfall.

When to go Skaftafell is accessible all year round. Popular paths can get overcrowded in summer. Glacier caves are only accessible October to March.

Planning ahead From July to August, book accommodation well in advance if you plan to overnight between Vík and Höfn.

Black Falls Most people have come across an image of the iconic **Svartifoss** waterfall before visiting Skaftafell – or even before visiting Iceland – so the actual site may be a little surprising: the waterfall is a stream, not a river, falling just 20m. But what it lacks in force is made up for by the spectacular basalt cliff, giving the waterfall an elegant picture frame. And as far as short hikes go, the 5km loop passing Svartifoss is one of the most pleasant walking experiences you could wish for.

The Hollywood glacier The name **Svínafellsjökull** may sound foreign, but for watchers of *Batman*, *Game of Thrones* and *James Bond* the glacial site is a familiar backdrop. The vista overlooking the glacier is halfway up a mountain and accessible on a short but bumpy gravel road about 2km east of the junction to Skaftafell. Rapid melting of

🌋 The Top of Iceland

At 2110m above sea level, the glacial **Hvannadalshnúkur** is Iceland's highest point. On clear days, the summit is visible from Skaftafell, a 12- to 18-hour hike away. Mountain Guides (mountainguides.is) and Tindaborg (tindaborg.is) run tours. Spring is the best time to go, when mornings are cold enough to keep the ice from thawing.

Above left Svínafellsjökull and surrounding mountains **Above right** Atlantic puffin **Left** Iconic Svartifoss

the glacier has increased the risk of landslides and falling rocks, limiting access beyond the vista.

Puffins at Ingólfshöfði Decades ago, pioneering the idea of organised tours, the farmer at Hofsnes began driving his tractor with a passenger-adjusted hay cart to the nearby **Cape Ingólfshöfði**. The cape has a spectacular sand beach and a rich history chronicling the arrival of Iceland's first settlers. From June to August puffins flock there to nest.

There are better places to spot puffins, but the birdlife adds to a wonderful 2½-hour experience guided by a local (fromcoastto-mountains.com).

Get the crampons on 'Glacier walks' are a popular way to explore the basics of glaciology. Over summer most tours take place on **Falljökull** (near Skaftafell) and during winter on **Breiðamerkurjökull** (near Jökulsárlón), lasting at least 2½ hours. Ice axe in hand, wearing massive crampons, guests are

🌋 Explore Europe's Largest Park

Fire meets ice at Vatnajökull National Park, with 10 active volcanoes – seven of them underneath the ice cap. The park is Europe's largest, covering 14% of Iceland. The southern Ring Rd from Kirkjubæjarklaustur to Lónsöræfi has many wonderful detours into the park, accessible only in summer:

Lakagígar Moss-grown and serene today, the volcanic craters at Laki formed in a 1783 eruption that killed a quarter of the Icelandic population.

Morsárjökull This remote valley glacier, accessible only on foot from Skaftafell, gives visual evidence of the shrinking of Vatnajökull's surface.

Lónsöræfi This trek from Lónsöræfi to Snæfell is a multi-day adventure.

Vatnajökull National Park
Vatnajökull
Hali
Breiðamerkurjökull
Bæjarstaðarskógur Forest
Kristinartindar
Jökulsárlón
Skaftafellsjökull Glacier
Svartifoss
Hvannadalshnúkur
Skaftafell
Svínafellsjökull
Svínafell
Falljökull
North Atlantic Ocean
Hof
Hnappavellir
Fagurhólsmýri
0 — 10 km
0 — 5 miles
Cape Ingólfshöfði

Left Moss-covered volcanic crater, Laki **Below** Ice cave, Vatnajökull glacier

guided to see cracks, streams and ponds forming on the glacier. The pace is slow and the difficulty modest; getting on the glacier from the moraine can be steep. (You won't need the ice axe, but it looks great in photos!)

Ice-blue caves Every winter, local 'ice-cavemen' go in their super-Jeeps to the foot of the Vatnajökull glacier searching for a natural entrance: the landscape changes every summer and is unsafe to visit outside the frozen months from October to March. The **Crystal Cave**, still used in some advertising, has been closed since 2019; instead the **Sapphire Cave** is a common destination but each tour depends on weather conditions and the number of sunlight hours. Tour operators include Arctic Adventures (adventures.is) and Local Guide of Vatnajökull (localguide.is). Expect to pay at least 30,000kr per person, since the massive trucks have limited seating.

Skaftafell on Foot

LOST IN A BIRCH FOREST? JUST STAND UP.

Skaftafell, a birch-tree forest at the base of the Vatnajökull glacier, is a rare peek into what Iceland may have been like during the medieval warm period that preceded settlement.

ANDRIY BLOKHIN/SHUTTERSTOCK ©

Historians debate *how* green Iceland was before settlement when a bunch of Norsemen arrived and practiced an unsustainable slash-and-burn agriculture on a landscape where soil forms slowly but erodes quickly. According to *The Book of Settlements*, the 13th-century chronicle penned by Iceland's earliest nerd, a man called Ari the Learned, the island was covered in trees 'from the coast to the mountains' – some contemporary studies claim as much as 30%.

The exact number depends a lot on the definition of 'tree'. The United Nations Agricultural Organization says anything under 5m is a bush! Grossly offended, Icelanders stand by their native junipers and woolly willows as trees – literally. They are human size.

'I love the calm', says local tour guide Sigurgeir Thoroddsen on a pleasant day in June, standing in front of the Skaftafell Visitor Centre with a busy parking lot and bathroom facilities for a thousand-plus visitors a day. The visitor centre doesn't look calm, but Thoroddsen insists: 'All you have to do is follow the trails *not* going to Svartifoss.'

The landmark Svartifoss waterfall is small but picturesque, with black basalt walls filling the frame, and no less impressive during the frozen winter. The 5km path from the parking lot is great and is suitable for all ages. On warm summer days, expect company.

Hikers seeking a day of solitude should head into the valley of Morsár glaicer or the Bæjarstaðaskógur forest; both paths are flat but long.

Amateur mountaineers, up for a challenge, can spend the day hiking up the Kristínartindar peaks. The stunning

Left Hikers brave the weather, Skaftafell **Middle** Footpath through summer foliage **Right** Iceland's iconic woolly willow

view at 1126m gives scale to the massive Vatnajökull glacier covering 8% of Iceland; the valley glaciers visible down on the ground are in fact just tiny outlets.

The Kristínartindar also offers an exclusive look at Iceland's highest waterfall, which streams down the Morsár glacier; the water flow has been powered by increased melting of the glacier, and in 2011 it was acknowledged as a single drop falling 228m – a waterfall, indeed. (Morsár waterfall takes the crown as Iceland's highest.) To manage expectations, the view is from a 6km distance.

> Icelanders stand by their native junipers and woolly willows as trees – literally. They are human size.

Looking towards the south, you will note the flip-side of climate change: young birch trees expanding over the once-grey glacial outwash. The self-seeded birch, native to Iceland, usually takes decades to grow but the warming of Iceland has prompted an unprecedented growth spurt. At the current rate, the area named after sand – Skeiðarársandur – will become the country's largest forest. That, says plant ecologist Kristín Svavarsdóttir, is among 'the most amazing developments currently taking place in Icelandic nature'.

In 2019, Skaftafell, along with most of Vatnajökull National Park, became a Unesco World Heritage Site precisely for its ephemeral landscape, a sort of lab, Unesco notes, to 'explore the impacts of climate change on world glaciers and the landforms left behind when they retreat'. The paths of Skaftafell will walk you through it.

Top Trails

Svartifoss–Sjónarsker–Sel Passing several waterfalls and an old farmhouse, this 5km loop is the most popular route. Allow 2½ hours.

Skaftafellsjökull Glacier The easiest trail available: some 2km on flat ground to a glacial moraine. Back the same way. Allow one to 1½ hours.

Bæjarstaðarskógur Forest Protected since 1935, this birch-tree forest is a wonderful 16km venture. Two beautiful ravines and long footbridges. Allow five hours.

Kristínartindar Mountain peaks with magnificent views. Bring an extra sweater and snacks – the hike is an 18km round-trip and takes six to eight hours depending on fitness and time of year. Consult with staff at the visitor centre before attempting this outside summer.

For maps and more, visit vatnajokulsthjodgardur.is.

18 Jökulsárlón
JAUNT

BOATING | KAYAKING | PHOTOGRAPHY

At Jökulsárlón glacier lagoon, Iceland lives up to its name: icebergs, calving from Europe's largest glacier, drift towards the sea and, almost there, they strand themselves on the sandbanks of the massive lagoon that was once entirely glacier.

LARIGAN · PATRICIA HAMILTON/GETTY IMAGES ©

How to

Getting there Route 1, the Ring Rd, crosses the southern tip of the lagoon where the largest icebergs are usually visible from the road. But park, please. The parking lot is massive.

When to go The soft evening sun, as well as early mornings, is a particularly lovely time to visit. Winter travellers may spot the Northern Lights – and get the ultimate Iceland picture.

Top tip The lagoon is home to ringed seals, sometimes seen resting on the ice.

WATEROTTER/GETTY IMAGES ©

SURANGAW/GETTY IMAGES ©

Points of entry Icebergs, big and small, line the southern end of the lagoon, furthest away from the Breiðamerkur glacier itself. Most visitors stop by the bridge, where the icebergs are closest to shore. But a little further west (called 'the alternative carpark' on Google Maps) are elevated paths with panoramic views.

Diamond Beach There was a time, in the not so distant past, when the small delta where the Jökulsárlón runs to the sea did not have a name. Now, inspired by some humble photo captions, the site goes by the name 'Diamond Beach'. This is a reference to the small pieces of ice that have floated up onto the beach, where they shine against charcoal-coloured sand.

Boating The trailer yachts driving up and down the shores of Jökulsárlón (since there is no harbour) are among the oldest businesses in Icelandic tourism. At the peak of summer, some 40 tours depart every day (icelagoon.is), cruising around the icebergs for 40 minutes. For double the price (11,000kr), a Zodiac driver will take you much closer to the glacier on a one-hour tour.

Kayaking The third option to explore the waters is by kayak (iceguide.is), also departing from the main parking lot. Reasonable fitness is required, as this activity lasts for roughly an hour (11,000kr per person). Unlike other transportation, kayaking is completely silent. Drip, drip, drip. Listen hard and you hear the water leave its frozen form.

Clockwise from bottom left Kayaker on Jökulsárlón; Jökulsárlón glacier lagoon; Diamond Beach

⛵ The Other Glacier Lagoon

Loners are generally out of luck when it comes to iceberg watching, such is its popularity. But the massive **Fjallsárlón** lagoon is less crowded than its famous neighbour. The area is private property, belonging to a nearby farm, which minimises the commercial chaos. It has only one cafe and one boating operator (fjallsarlon.is), which offers 45-minute dinghy excursions. Due to the lagoon's depth, the icebergs are more spread out than in Jökulsárlón, with fewer opportunities for a close-range sighting from land.

Glaciers

THE (EVER-RETREATING) FRONTLINE OF CLIMATE CHANGE

Iceland is roughly 10% ice – unless this guidebook is being read long after publication: every year glacial land twice the size of Keflavík Airport disappears. Few frozen regions on the planet are as accessible to travellers, but keeping the glaciers alive goes beyond preserving a natural attraction.

Left Entrance to ice cave, Vatnajökull glacier **Middle** Icebergs from Breiðamerkur glacier **Right** Skaftafellsjökull glacier

Back in 1995, when Gudfinna Adalgeirsdóttir finished her PhD in glaciology, climate change was in popular discourse a punchline at best. 'Our summers are balmy, but we have high hopes for that global warming', whimsical Icelanders would tell visitors. Even the weather reporter on television would describe hot days as 'soon running Iceland out of business'.

These jokes are no longer in good taste. Almost half of the total glacial melt Iceland has witnessed since the Little Ice Age has occurred within the last 30 years, roughly the span of Adalgeirsdóttir's career.

'I knew. Scientists knew', she says in her matter-of-fact manner. 'But I can lay out the facts more firmly today.' For one, the satellite images of today are impossible to argue: a time-lapse of Ok glacier shows a white circle in the western highlands fade, decade by decade, year by year, into a tiny dot. Dead. In 2019, a funeral was held for Ok, the first glacier to lose its status.

The other 15 ice caps could go the same way, and the smaller most definitely will. Under the Paris Climate Agreement, a policy framework meant to keep temperatures from rising 2°C above pre-industrial levels, the mighty Vatnajökull glacier, up to 1km in thickness, will still shrink to 30% to 60% of its current size.

For the people of Iceland, a world without ice brings more than just an identity crisis. Waning glaciers lead to a phenomena named 'crustal uplift' – similar to when a heavy object is removed from a mattress; the nearby surface springs up. In the town of Höfn, where Vatnajökull is close and visible, land rises by about 2cm each year, twisting the town's sewer pipes. The town's iconic

harbour has already grown too shallow for large ships to use during low tide.

Roughly 70% of electricity in Iceland is produced with hydroelectric power plants in rivers streaming from the glaciers. As the glacial melt increases, the rivers grow more powerful, producing ever more electricity. But only for the time being. The state-run energy company Landsvirkjun is installing more wind turbines to prepare for a looming energy shift.

> Almost half of the total glacial melt Iceland has witnessed since the Little Ice Age has occurred within the last 30 years.

Tourism is booming in the Arctic, a trend attributed to the desire to see our frozen planet before it changes.

Iceland, a relatively easy place to get to, has most of its major glacial sites concentrated south of Vatnajökull; the popular Jökulsárlón lagoon is within the range of an electric car from Reykjavík – and has a charging station on the parking site. The Breiðamerkur glacier, calving into the lagoon, covered the parking lot one hundred years ago.

Jökulsárlón is altogether about 20 sq km, half the size of Iceland's annual loss of glacial land over the past decade.

The icebergs drift across the lagoon and run aground on the southern side, conveniently next to the Ring Rd. All lined up for a photograph, they melt, break and roll around. It's as if they are calling our attention to something...

🥾 The Melting Glacier Walk

Every afternoon, June to August, the Vatnajökull National Park offers a guided tour to the Skaftafellsjökull glacier. Free of charge, the hour-long walk starts at the Skaftafell Visitor Centre, approximately where the glacier used to be at the dawn of the 20th century. Tour leader Ari Másson says guests walk through the glacier's past; the trail enters moraines where the oldest hills date to the 1930s. 'Put into perspective, the landscape is shocking to most people', he says. A small lagoon now separates the walking path from the glacier's edge; the tour turns around on the highest sandhill, after some 2km of walking. Visit vatnajokulsthjodgardur.is/en/learn/programs-and-events for timetables, or ask at the visitor centre. (If you can't make the walk, the route is marked 'S1' on the trail map.)

19 Eastern VILLAGES

FRESH FISH | QUIRKY MUSEUMS | LOCAL ART

Home to fishers and farmers, hotels and aluminium smelters, an artist commune and a finishing school, the villages of the East embody the contrasts of Icelandic life. It's a region where people can tell cod from haddock and welcome visitors: the local *austfirðingar* are chatty at the local baths and eager for guests to try their speciality reindeer burger with a milkshake or a Breiðdalsvík brew.

🗺 How to

Getting around Mountain tunnels make driving distances relatively short between the larger towns known collectively as Fjarðabyggð. The road to Mjóifjörður (population 11) is often closed in winter and the pass to Seyðis-fjörður can be hazardous.

When to go Most places stay open year-round, although with limited opening hours over winter.

Top tip Seyðisfjörður Church hosts concerts every Wednesday night from July to August with a fabulous line-up of prominent musicians.

Top Seyðisfjörður **Bottom** Petra's Mineral Collection, Stöðvarfjörður

The artist colony **Seyðisfjörður** is a port town turned artist colony. With old timber houses painted in the colours of the rainbow, this charming town is best explored on a stroll. Starting from the blue church, several arts-and-crafts boutiques line the road to **Skaftfell Culture Centre** (skaftfell.is), a stronghold for visual artists that also, conveniently, serves pizza. At the edge of Seyðisfjörður is the walk-in sound sculpture Tvísöngur, well worth the 15-minute walk uphill from the Brimberg Fish Factory. In 2020, a massive landslide destroyed part of the town, explaining the multiple construction projects.

Fish, straight from the pan The furthest town from Reykjavík, **Neskaupstaður** can sustain almost every desire of a modern cosmopolitan life despite its remoteness – or perhaps because of it. There is even a fabulous record store. One of the country's largest fishing companies is based here; to taste the catch of the day head to Beitiskúrinn (Bait Shack), which offers an outside setting on a wharf and fried fish served directly on a black skillet.

Cold lake, hot bath Since opening in 2019, the top-of-the-line **Vök Baths** (vokbaths.is) has been a default destination for those seeking to soak in hot water at the edge of a cold lake. It's an architectural delight with a swim-up bar serving a selection of colourful teas. Located 5km from the regional capital of Egilsstaðir.

🏛 New Village, New Museum

Each eastern village prides itself on a landmark museum with a theme that draws out the character of its community. **Fáskrúðsfjörður** has the French Museum honouring the 19th-century legacy of French sailors; **Eskifjörður** the Maritime Museum in a wooden house from 1816; **Reyðarfjörður** the neatly located Wartime Museum covering occupation of Allied forces in WWII. But the most intriguing of all is at a private home in **Stöðvarfjörður**, where Petra's Mineral Collection (steinapetra.is) displays hundreds of colourful rocks. Stone collector Petra Sveinsdottir (1922–2012) began welcoming guests around 1975, soon after her husband passed away, and today the collection is maintained by her four children.

20 Eastern **ESCAPE**

HIKES | KAYAKING | ROAD TRIP

Ever since the days of early typography, the Eastfjords (which, roughly speaking, extend from Djúpivogur in the south to Vopnafjörður in the north) have been marked with vague lines of guesswork. To this day, the region remains Iceland's least explored. And that's precisely its charm.

🗺 How to

Getting around The stunning Rte 939, known as Öxi, is a shortcut to Egilsstaðir over summer. Winter snow shuts gravel roads.

When to go Planning to jump into the river Eyvindará, like the locals on sunny days?

Then summer is probably best. Otherwise, take your pick.

Before you leave To realise your potential as a Nordic strongman, try to lift the 186kg boulder outside the swimming pool in Egilsstaðir.

The dancefloor cave Whether the **Easter Cave** (Páskahellir), located on a rocky beach in the Neskaupstaður Nature Reserve, is a cove or a small cave is debatable. Either way, this quiet spot is a favourite among locals. Getting there is 20 minutes on foot, each way, and the walk simply starts where the road ends a few kilometres east of Neskaup- staður. From the cave 'one can watch the sun dance on Easter morning', a signpost claims, without elaborating on what that means exactly.

This way, Indiana Jones About a 10-minute drive from the town of Eskifjörður is a hole in the ground that once changed the world. It's the entry to the 70m-long **Helgustaða Mine**, where the largest and purest crystals to project light were once found. These led to the invention of telescopes and magnifiers.

Reindeerland

In the early 18th century, the Icelandic government import- ed reindeers and set them free for the benefit of sustain- able game hunting. The same thing was tried with musk ox, native to Greenland. What remains of these experiments are the 3000 reindeers living solely in the East and often visible from the road – if not crossing the lanes!

Clockwise from left Reindeer; Stuðlagil canyon; Páskahellir, the dancefloor cave

Known as Iceland Spar, the biggest chunk ever extracted is in fact on display at the British Natural History Museum. Today, only small pieces remain left at the site. Bring a flashlight and note the old railway tracks.

To the kayaks! Paddlers are in paradise in the calm eastern fjords. In Neskaupstaður, the local kayaking club **Kaj** (facebook.com/kajakklubburinnkaj) rents out equipment and 'sometimes' offers guided trips. Best to have some level of experience.

Old rocks, new view Although inland, and strictly speaking not part of the Eastfjords, nearby **Stuðlagil canyon** is a must-see destination. Its magnificent basalt formations existed, unseen, for hundreds of centuries. The explanation: the gigantic Kárahnjúkar Hydropower Plant dammed the glacier river streaming through the canyon. As the water level shrunk, basalt banks of unusual height and with streaks of earthy colours were revealed.

⚠ The Five-Summit Challenge

In 2020, local mountaineers placed stamps on top of the region's five iconic mountains: Kistufell, Hólmatindur, Svartafjall, Goðaborg, Hádegisfjall. Collect all five stamps in a special pamphlet (500kr) and you have earned the title 'Fjallagarpur Fjarðamanna' – the Mountaineer of the Fjords. Respect!

How long will it take? Well, altogether the five summits are 5186m; roughly the equivalent of Mont Blanc.

So you may not have time! But this is all to say: the East is for hiking. For ideas, check out the booklet *The Pearls of Egilsstaðir Area*, published by the local touring club. It has 30 excellent hiking suggestions, long and short. Free online at visitegilsstadir.is.

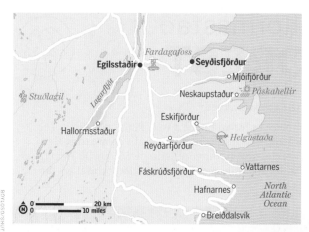

THE EAST & SOUTHEAST EXPERIENCES

Left Hólmatindur, one of the region's five iconic mountains **Below** Fardagafoss

It is possible to access the canyon from both sides of the river Jökulsá á Dal. The view is arguably better from the eastern side starting by the Klaustursel farm. Before crossing the bridge, guests are asked to park their car in the parking lot. From there, walk on the gravel road past a small waterfall and sheep barn, and then on to a path. Altogether 5km, one way.

Alternatively, the vista on the western side requires almost no walking. To get there, continue past Klaustursel on the road Jökuldalsvegur and look for the Stuðlagil sign. Cars are parked pretty much on the cliff's edge.

Get behind this On the road to Seyðisfjörður, the **Fardagafoss** may seem like yet another waterfall. But look closer and there is a cave. The narrow entry is a wet adventure, but what else to expect when going behind a waterfall? The sound of water falling some 20m blasts the cave, and if outlaws still existed, there would certainly be one hiding in there.

21 Hallormsstaður
FOREST

FOREST TRAILS | WATERFALL | LOCAL HARVEST

█████ Welcome to the best place in Iceland to be a tree. Pine. Oak. Birch. The Hallormsstaður Forest is Iceland's largest, with hiking trails showcasing the surprising number of tree species able to thrive at latitude 65° north. Sometimes called 'the least Icelandic landscape', this is an area where local travellers far outnumber foreign tourists.

OLEG SENKOV/SHUTTERSTOCK ©

🗺 How to

Getting around The forest has 11 paths, covering 740 hectares. Maps are available at parking lots and Hotel Hallormsstaður, as well as online (visitegilsstadir.is).

When to go June to August. Summer solstice, around 21 June, is celebrated with a bonfire and the oddly exciting Lumberjack National Championship.

Top tip The Orkan gas station is a de facto ice-cream store!

SASHAGAF/SHUTTERSTOCK ©

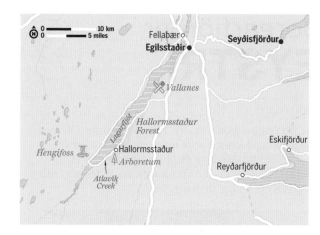

Fellabær
Egilsstaðir
Seyðisfjörður
Vallanes
Hallormsstaður Forest
Lagarfljót
Hengifoss
Hallormsstaður
Arboretum
Eskifjörður
Reyðarfjörður
Atlavík Creek

Stroll the arboretum On a hot summer day, the pristine **Atlavík Creek** is hot property for tents and campervans. This is where Icelanders go on vacation. (And just watch how quickly guests leave at the sign of clouds, off to a sunnier corner of the country.) From the parking lot, take a pleasant 2km path to the arboretum containing 80 tree species, following the cliffs of Lagarfljót river. Plenty of excellent picnic spots.

Sheep sorrel pesto at Vallanes To get a delicious taste of this fertile region, and a sense for the practical use of forestry, visit **Vallanes farm**, which offers pancakes made from locally grown barley, homemade veggie burgers and pesto made of wild sheep sorrel. The restaurant (modirjord.is) is built entirely of local wood. Apple trees grow outside as part a bold sub-Arctic experiment, and purple grapes hang inside a colourful greenhouse.

Third-tallest waterfall The 128m **Hengifoss** was once Iceland's second-tallest waterfall, but lost its place when the melting Morsár glacier snapped the first seat. But silver or bronze, it's still much loved! Located at the top of a canyon, getting here is part of the fun. The pleasant path is about a 5km round-trip and only moderately steep. Allow 1½ to two hours and keep an eye out for the magnificent basalt rocks by the smaller Litlanes waterfall midway.

Top Banks of the Lagarfljót **Bottom** Pine cone

〰 The Lagarfljót Wyrm

Tempted to go for a swim in the calm river Lagarfljót with its inviting stony creeks? Think again. This wide river is fed by a murky glacial stream, making it cold and deep. And somewhere near the bottom, at 110m, swims the Lagarfljót Wyrm. This folkloric figure is arguably Iceland's most famous monster, first chronicled in a 1350 script and regularly spotted since. In the winter of 2012, a retired farmer on his afternoon walk caught the creature on camera. The internet has the proof.

22 Borgarfjörður EYSTRI

BIRDWATCHING | HIKING | SOLITUDE

The puffins are stoic. The stones home to elfs. The village from a bygone age. Borgarfjörður Eystri is a hiking destination of quiet energy, in a remote fjord an hour's drive from the Ring Rd. Walking distances range from 15 minutes (the harbour birdcliff) to five days (the Víknaslóðir trail), but regardless of route most people end up staying longer than expected.

📷 How to

Getting there At the time of writing, Rd 94 was being paved all the way to the village of Bakkagerði (population 77) and its two hotels. The construction will open the area up to winter visitors, but check road conditions (road.is) for the Vatnsskarð mountain pass during the months of snow.

When to go June to early August for the birdlife.

Top tip The Musteríð Spa, located in the old fish factory, has three multi-temperature hot tubs with stunning views.

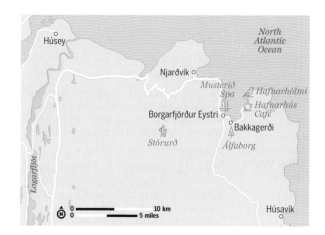

Puffinland Some 7km from Bakkagerði village is a harbour where, during the summer, you'll find hard-at-work fishers. The grassy rock of **Hafnarhólmi**, which shelters the harbour, is one of the best places on Iceland's mainland to see puffins up close. Along with fulmars and kittiwakes, the puffins nest in the Hafnarhólmi colony from June to August when the baby pufflings can survive on their own. Before leaving, see if the **Hafnarhús Café** is open. You won't miss the building; it's a three store 'harbour house' showcasing the latest (minimalist) trends in Nordic architecture.

Hidden boulders A middle-of-nowhere lagoon of giant boulders, **Stórurð** is the highlight of the alpine Dyrfjöll mountain ridge. This pristine place owes its atmospheric beauty to how hard it is to get here: allow four to six hours for a round-trip depending on your level of fitness. That said, the walk is relatively easy and flat, as the trail starts several hundred metres up on the Vatnsskarð pass on Rd 94. Hiking boots are recommended to handle the gravel terrain, unless you are training for the annual Dyrfjalla Run, a notoriously challenging trail run held in July.

Meet the elves The rocky hill above the local campground is called **Álfaborg** – the City of Elves – and according to folklore a visit brings good luck. At the very least, the hill has an excellent vista. The local church down the hill is usually open, and it's worth checking out the peculiar **altarpiece**; it depicts Jesus giving his 'Sermon on the Mount' on top of the Álfaborg hill and is one of the earliest works of legendary painter Jóhannes Kjarval, who grew up on a poor sheep farm nearby.

Top View from the Víknaslóðir trail
Bottom A puffin takes flight

🥾 Víknaslóðir Trail

The marked 55km trail from Borgarfjörður Eystri to Seyðisfjörður, known as Víknaslóðir, has over recent years become an increasingly popular alternative to the well-established highland routes like Landmannalaugar and Lónsöræfi. Here hikers travel in solitude. The route covers three landmark creeks – Brúnavík, Breiðavík and Húsavík – and can be done in three to five days depending on the destination. Most hikers end in the deserted Loðmundar Fjord and get a jeep-ride back to Bakkagerði; others add an extra day and end in the town of Seyðisfjörður.

Listings

BEST OF THE REST

Hot Baths

Selárdalslaug

Built on the banks of a salmon river in 1949, Selárdalslaug is a sudden surprise on the empty road north of Vopnafjörður. This part of Iceland has little geothermal heating, making it all the more unique and appreciated.

Hornafjörður Swimming Pool

Blue, red and yellow – the three waterslides at this swimming pool in Höfn offer serious rides. Hot tubs are nice, too.

Eskifjörður Swimming Pool

Three multi-temperature tubs (for the lazy) and two waterslides (for the crazy). And a 25m pool for swimming. Perfecto.

Djúpavogskörin

South of the village of Djúpivogur, on a random geothermal field, are two hot tubs, built by locals seeking to unwind and socialise. Anyone can visit; just treat this communal property with respect. No locker facilities.

Fresh Coffee, Traditional Atmosphere

Hjáleigan Kaffihús

Located outside a turf house hosting the Bustarfell Museum near Vopnafjörður, this cafe serves impressive homemade cakes from traditional recipes. Try the rhubarb pie called *hjónabandssæla* (happy marriage cake).

Nesbær

The bakery in Neskaupstaður is also a shop for a good yarn. Friendly staff, good vibes and a cinnamon bun to go with it – you will leave knowing a little more about local life.

Kaupfjelagið Verzlun

Part cafe, part grocery in Breiðdalsvík, with an air of nostalgia. The store matches the look of the town's old general store, with packed wooden shelves and a fancy cashier table.

Fjalladýrð

The wooden Fjalladýrð – built from local trees, driftwood and a telephone pole – is on the Ring Rd junction to Möðrudalur, the country's highest inhabited farm. Don't miss the homemade *kleinur* (twisted doughnuts).

Seafood

Randulff's Seahouse €€

In a wooden house showcasing artefacts from the time Eskifjörður was a herring base, this seafood restaurant is a top place to taste East Iceland. Outside seating on the water, and if you fancy catching the fish yourself the restaurant has a boat!

Café Sumarlina €€

In a landmark wooden house, this restaurant in Fáskrúðsfjörður has a family-friendly menu of fish and chips, pizzas and burgers.

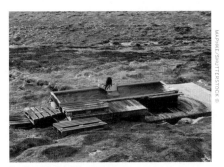

Geothermal hot tub, Djúpavogskörin

Hafnarbúðin   €

Höfn's old harbour diner, serving burgers, milkshakes and most famously a langoustine baguette – with lots of mayo.

Pakkhús Restaurant   €€€

The restaurant in Höfn specialises in 'Icelandic lobster' – technically langoustine – caught by fishers working at the nearby harbour.

🖼 Outdoor Art

Eggin í Gleðivík

A 1km stroll from the village of Djúpivogur, artist Sigurður Guðmundsson has placed 34 egg-shaped rocks to represent local bird species. As with any good art, reviews are mixed.

The Red Chair

By the Ring Rd, next to the Þorgeirsstaðir farm between Höfn and Djúpivogur, is a red chair of gigantic size. Keep it warm for the troll and enjoy this picturesquely situated furniture.

The Phone Booth in Seyðisfjörður

At the edge of Seyðisfjörður is a mysterious phone booth titled *How Are Things...?* Made in 2006 by artist Guðjón Ketilsson the booth marked the hundred-year anniversary of a submarine telegraph cable from Scotland being brought ashore at Seyðisfjörður.

🎪 Festival Fun

LungA

LungA Art Festival is an art and music festival drawing big names to Seyðisfjörður every July since 2000. A wonderfully diverse celebration of all things art.

Eistnaflug Metal Festival

The Eistnaflug Metal Festival is held in Neskaupstaður during the second weekend of July and attracts international bands and metalheads. Wondering if this is for you? Try the Icelandic band Skálmöld.

A stretch of road along the Vattarnes peninsula

Fjarðabyggð on Foot

The late-June hiking festival, Á fætur í Fjarðabyggð, is a week-long schedule of guided walks. For more, visit fjardabyggd.is and use the search term 'gönguvikan'.

🚗 Summer Detours

Hellisheiði Eystri

How steep is a 12% slope? Hellisheiði Eystri, on Rte 917 between Egilsstaðir and Vopnafjörður, is the highest mountain pass still in wide use.

Vattarnes

Instead of taking the tunnel between Fáskrúðsfjörður and Reyðarfjörður, Rte 955 along the Vattarnes peninsula is a gravel road with wonderful views and sheep casually crossing the road.

Mjóifjörður

An hour-long zigzag on a gravel road into a fjord that is home to a community of 11 people. Over winter, the road usually closes. Check out the Klifbrekku waterfall and stop for coffee at Brekka.

Scan to find more things to do in the East online

AKUREYRI

SKIING | SPLASHING | SAVOURING

Experience
Akureyri
online

AKUREYRI
Trip Builder

This little big town is a centre for outdoor activities in all seasons: nature exploration, hiking, water sports – and skiing. It also has a vibrant cultural scene, and opportunities for après-ski are aplenty.

Explore bookable experiences in **Akureyri** online

Listen to live Icelandic music at **Græni hatturinn** (p165)
🕐 ½ day

Find your balance paddleboarding in the **Akureyri harbour** (p167)
🕐 ½ day

Hike **Súlur** for a splendid view of the town (p167)
🕐 ½ day

Try the varied slopes at **Hlíðarfjall** ski resort (p163)
🕐 ½–1 day

Explore Eyjafjarðarsveit and quirky museum **Smámuna-safnið** (p161)
🕐 ½–1 day

Myrkarjökull

Hörgá

Strýta

Hraundrangi

Háls ○

Háafjall

Akureyri

Eyjafjarðará

Hrafnagil

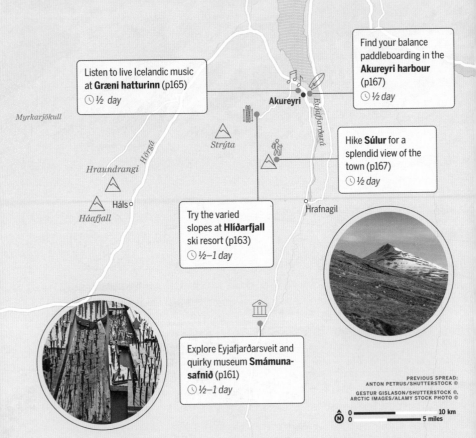

Ⓝ 0 ────── 10 km
0 ──── 5 miles

Practicalities

ARRIVING

Akureyri Airport Rent a car, take a taxi or walk into town (30 minutes).

Hof Buses from Reykjavík go to the Hof bus stop in downtown Akureyri. The taxi station (BSO) and (free) public bus station are within a five-minute walk.

FIND YOUR WAY

There's no tourist information centre but travel advice is available on visitakureyri.is.

MONEY

Cards are widely accepted; there are ATMs downtown. Buy food at supermarkets and pack lunches to save money.

WHERE TO STAY

Town	Pro/Con
Camping, glamping	Two campgrounds – one in town, one on the outskirts. In Eyjafjarðarsveit you can sleep in a yurt.
Hostels, hotels, guesthouses	Several to choose from; varying price ranges and amenities.
Cottages, apartments	With cooking facilities; located inside or outside town.
Farmstay	Outside town; country atmosphere.

EATING & DRINKING

Local institution Bautinn Restaurant (pictured) has operated since 1971. Seek out lamb or fish on the varied menu.

Cocktails Sip cocktails on the porch overlooking the downtown at Múlaberg Bistro & Bar.

Coffee and cake Find good coffee and cakes at Kaffi Ilmur (pictured). Also offers fabulous lunch and brunch buffets.

Must-try bakery Helgi Magri's Food Trail (p161)
Best rooftop view R5 (p166)

GETTING AROUND

Walking Most places are walkable, but some streets are steep.

Taxi Operate from BSO in the town centre.

Bus The Akureyri bus (straeto.is/en/timatoflur/5) is free. All routes begin and end by the main stop (Miðbær) in the city centre.

AKUREYRI FIND YOUR FEET

JAN–MAR
Resort ski season. Short days, dark nights. Northern Lights.

APR–JUN
Off-piste ski season. Long days, bright nights. Midnight sun.

JUL–SEP
Best for hiking, wildlife watching, outdoors.

OCT–DEC
Storms, winter road conditions. Short days, Northern Lights.

23 Adventure in EYJAFJÖRÐUR

FOOD | FARMS | NATURE

▬▬▬▬ A few kilometres south of Akureyri, framed by tall mountains, lies the rural paradise of Eyjafjarðarsveit. Locals love it for weekend drives and cycling trips, farmhouse cafes, quirky shops and museums and rejuvenating in nature.

ALGMIER PHOTOGRAPHY/SHUTTERSTOCK ©

📖 How to

Getting around Bring your own bike or hire a car at Akureyri Airport. There are no public bus services.

When to go Year-round but summer is especially lovely and is when most services are open. A local handicraft festival, Handverkshátíð, is held in Hrafnagil in early August.

Where to stay You can overnight at a farm, in your own tent, a yurt, or an old-fashioned farmhouse. (esveit.is/ferdathjonusta/gisting)

VISIONDREAMS / 500PX/GETTY IMAGES ©

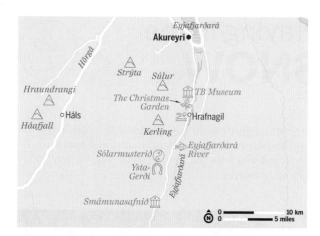

Active and relaxing hiking At 1538m, **Kerling** is North Iceland's tallest mountain. An unmarked hiking path leads up the mountain from Finnastaðir (Rd 824) down to Glerárdalur valley on the other side. The path is steep and only for hikers in good shape (and in good weather). From the top there are views of the highlands and all the way to Vatnajökull glacier.

Angling Eyjafjarðará river is known for big Arctic char. Fishing permits are online (sala.eyjafjardara.is/permits/eyjafjardara).

Riding Go horse riding at **Ysta-Gerði** (ysta-gerdi.com).

Yoga At **Sólarmusterið** (solarmusterid.is) join peace walks, storytelling and yogic events. **Retreat Inspiration Iceland** (inspiration-iceland.com) offers yoga classes, treatments, tours and hikes.

Swimming The swimming pool at **Hrafnagil** has a fun water-slide and is great for families. Opposite Akureyri with a view of town and fjord are the newly constructed 'Forest Baths' (p197).

The curious, cute and quirky Kristnes is where the region's first settler built his home. Later it became a tuberculosis healing centre. Walk around the Kristnes forest and visit the **TB museum** (haelid.is). **The Christmas Garden** attracts visitors in all seasons, but especially around the holidays. The gingerbread cookie house carries kitsch, candy and collectables. **Smámunasafnið** showcases a local eccentric's amazing collection of tools, pencils, rusty nails and anything you can think of! The cafe serves old-fashioned countryside treats. Iceland's answer to Europe's gothic cathedrals are tiny **countryside churches**. Eyjafjarðarsveit has six.

Top Eyjafjarðará river **Bottom** Icelandic horses

🏬 On the Food Trail

Eyjafjarðarsveit is a centre for dairy production, but the region's farmers also produce beef, lamb, pork, horse meat, eggs and honey, and grow potatoes and greenhouse vegetables. Local food producers and caterers have joined forces to form **Helgi Magri's Food Trail** (facebook.com/matars-tigurhelgamagra). Taste farm-made ice cream at Holtsel, watch the cows being milked at Kaffi Kú, attend a horse show at Brúnir Horse, learn more about local food and visit the other participants in the project.

24 Playing in the SNOW

SKIING | ADVENTURE | FAMILY

In and around Akureyri the skiing season may last from mid-November to mid-June. Hit the slopes with your family, ski under the stars and Northern Lights, ski under the midnight sun and from the summit to the sea. Or don't ski at all and opt for sledding or snowshoeing.

ELLI THOR MAGNUSSON/GETTY IMAGES ©

🗺 **How to**

Getting here It's easiest to hire a car. Bus 78 (straeto.is) runs between the main skiing towns. Some slopes and tracks can be reached on foot.

When to go December to March for alpine and cross-country skiing at the resorts. March to May for the main off-piste ski season.

How much Five-resort pass costs adult/child 23,400/8100kr. A day pass in Akureyri ski resort costs adult/child 5600/1600kr. Ski and snowboard rentals cost around adult/child 3900/1900kr.

VITALALP/GETTY IMAGES ©

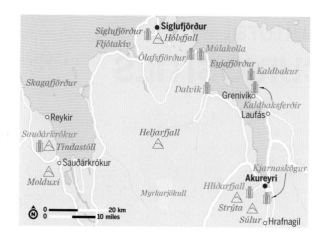

Take Your Pick

Alpine skiing Hlíðarfjall in Akureyri is the largest resort with varied lifts and slopes and ski lessons for children and adults. Dalvík is half an hour to the north, and another 30-minute drive will take you to Ólafsfjörður and Siglufjörður. Sauðárkrókur is one hour on. The resorts vary in size and levels of service, but all have groomed pistes for alpine skiing and snowboarding. (skiiceland.is)

Cross-country skiing Find tracks in and around Kjarnaskógur in Akureyri (open for all) and at all the resorts. Sometimes there are tracks in Skíðadalur near Dalvík (no charge). Courses are offered in Ólafsfjörður and Siglufjörður (email siglohotel@siglohotel.is for availability).

Mountain skiing There are off-piste opportunities at the resorts. Mountains Kaldbakur and Múlakolla are popular for off-piste skiing. Arctic Freeride (facebook.com/arcticfreeride) and Kaldbaksferðir (kaldbaksferdir.com/contact) offer snowcat tours. For info on ski touring and heli-skiing, go to bergmenn.com, vikingheliskiing.com and arcticheliskiing.com.

Snowshoeing For a slower-paced winter adventure, go to wideopen.is and siglohotel.is.

Sledding Kaldbaksferðir offer snowcat and sledding tours for families. In Akureyri, locals go to Jólasveinabrekkan for sledding (no charge; parking in Brálundur).

Top Children sledding, Mývatn
Bottom Snowshoeing at sunrise

❄ Winter Festivals

Mývatn Winter Festival

Held in March, the festival is packed with special events like horseback riding on ice. It also features dog sledding, snowmobiling, cross-country skiing and ice fishing. (vetrarhatid.com)

Iceland Winter Games

Also in March, Akureyri hosts a freeskiing competition and lots of other snow-filled events, like snowskating, downhill snow-bike racing and snow volleyball. (iceland-wintergames.com)

Cultural
CURIOSITIES

ART | MUSIC | HISTORY

▬▬▬ Take it slow and explore a different side to Akureyri. Spend a few hours meadering through the art, history and heritage museums, immerse yourself in the lives and works of the town's authors and poets, listen to live music and enjoy a night on the town.

How to

Getting around Most museums, clubs and cultural institutions are within walking distance. The public buses are free. You can also take a taxi or hire a car.

When to go June to August is when the main cultural festivals take place. A performance festival is held in October. Many concerts are scheduled around Christmas and Easter.

Top tip At Akureyri Museum in Innbærinn you can buy a pass for five museums and learn about the town's history and cultural events. (minjasafnid.is)

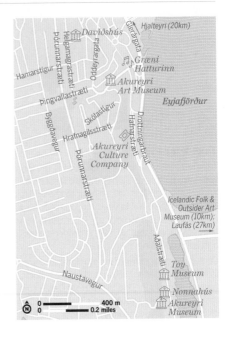

Art Inside old industrial buildings in the 'Arts Alley', **Akureyri Art Museum** showcases the works of local and national artists. The cosy museum cafe serves good coffee, cakes and wine. A 20-minute drive north lies the hamlet of **Hjalteyri**, where an art centre operates inside an old herring factory in the summer. On the other side of Eyjafjörður, a giant 'curator' greets visitors to the **Icelandic Folk and Outsider Art Museum**.

History The **Akureyri Museum** is a complex of museums. The main building on Aðalstræti 58 has rotating exhibitions on the town's history and everyday life. **Nonnahús**, the house where children's book author Jón Sveinsson (Nonni) used to

Top Hof Cultural Center **Bottom** Horseshoes and tools, Laufás

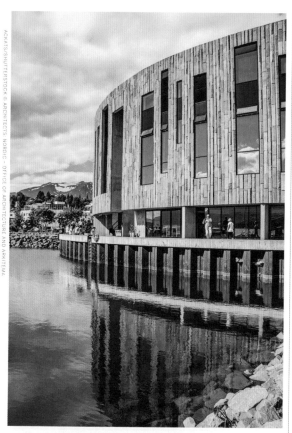

❄ Akureyri Art Summer

The long-standing festival Listasumar (Akureyri Art Summer) is held through the month of July. The festival includes an array of events for all ages and appetites: pop, rock and classical concerts, visual-art exhibitions, outdoor art and workshops. (listasumar.is)

live, has been preserved like a time capsule. Also visit the **Toy Museum**; **Davíðshús**, the house of poet Davíð Stefánsson; and stately turf farm **Laufás** on the other side of the fjord. The museum organises concerts, history walks and the annual Medieval Days at Gásir.

Music The **Akureyri Culture Company** represents the Akureyri Theatre Company, North Iceland Symphonic Orchestra and the Hof Cultural Center. In the landmark building by the harbour, shows, concerts and conferences are held. Classical concerts are often held at Easter. Unassuming **Græni hatturinn**, in the basement cafe of Bláa kannan in the town centre, is the busiest concert venue in Iceland.

Listings

BEST OF THE REST

 ## Parks & Forests

Public Park & Botanic Garden

The small park is at its loveliest from June to September. Stroll among the trees and flowers, have picnics and attend events, or enjoy a slice of cake at the cafe. In sunny weather, kids like to cool off in the fountain.

Kjarnaskógur

Another local favourite is Kjarnaskógur forest with walking paths and bridges across a bubbly stream, playgrounds, communal BBQs and a beach volleyball court.

Vaglaskógur

About 30-minutes' drive through the Vaðlaheiði tunnel lies one of Iceland's largest forests. Nearby is petting zoo Daladýrð, where kids can jump in the hay!

Akureyri Golf Club

Play golf at Jaðarsvöllur, the world's northern most 18-hole golf course. The Arctic Open is held annually in late June where golfers compete under the midnight sun.

 ## Art & Design

Vorhús

Established by designer Sveinbjörg Hallgrímsdóttir, Vorhús is popular for its cups, bedsheets and other objects featuring designs inspired by Icelandic landscapes.

Íslensk.is

In a historical house by the harbour, designer Hugrún Ívarsdóttir runs a store carrying various products, including tablecloths and platters with *laufabrauð* patterns, inspired by the North Icelandic Christmas bread.

 ## Foreign Flavours

Kurdo Kebab   €

Serves shawarma, falafel and other treats to hungry night owls and other guests.

Indian Curry House   €€

Locals love the kormas, curries and tikka masalas so much this restaurant had to move to a bigger location on the town square.

Orðakaffi   €€

At the public library, Italian-style Orðakaffi serves scrumptious lunch buffets, sourdough bread and tempting cakes. Good coffee too.

 ## Beer, Draught & Craft

R5

At this micro bar you'll find the largest variety of beer in North Iceland, local and otherwise. Groups can book beer and food pairings.

Backpackers

The hostel-cum-restaurant offers a selection of Icelandic beer, mass produced and micro brewed, along with no-fuss food and advice.

Public Park & Botanic Garden

Ölstofa Akureyrar

In the 'Arts Alley' you'll find the local Einstök Brewery's tasting lounge with eight types of beer on draught and lots more in bottles.

Oceanic Adventures

Paddle North Iceland & Venture North

Based at Akureyri Harbour, these companies offer paddleboarding tours on Eyjafjörður. The former focuses on families; the latter on SUP.

Hjalteyri Kayak Rental & Nonni Travel

These companies offer sea-kayaking tours on Eyjafjörður. The former are family friendly, with fishing tours (and whale watching) and a hot tub afterwards. The latter specialises in longer tours from Grenivík past seabird cliffs.

Fairytale at Sea

The Ólafsfjörður-based company offers jet-ski tours to places usually hidden from view, in the shadow of mighty mountains surrounded by sea birds and breaching whales.

Strýtan Divecenter & Arctic Trip

Both companies offer diving and snorkelling tours. The former, based in Hjalteyri, takes experienced divers to the unique geothermal chimneys in Eyjafjörður. The latter, based on Grímsey island, offers diving and snorkelling.

Whale-Watching Hauganes

From tiny Hauganes, join a whale-watching tour of Eyjafjörður with optional sea angling. The local restaurant serves varied fish dishes and there are hot tubs at the beach.

Surfing

With world-class waves, Ólafsfjörður is a hotspot for surfers.

Humpback whale near Hauganes

Hiking & Nature Walks

Leiran & the Eyjafjarðará Delta

Find walking paths south of Akureyri Airport and a birdwatching house. Bring a stick as protection from Arctic tern attacks.

Krossanesborgir

A nature reserve on the outskirts of Akureyri with walking paths between boulders, a pond, diverse plants and birdlife, and a narrow beach.

Glerárdalur

Follow river Glerá, which runs through Akureyri, into Glerárdalur. A 10km path leads from the parking space on Súluvegur to the valley's end.

Fálkafell & Súlur

For a splendid view of Akureyri, the fjord and surrounding mountains, head to Fálkafell. For a more challenging hike summit Súlur.

Hraunsvatn

At the foot of the eerie Hraundrangi mountain range in Öxnadalur, is this hidden gem of a lake. Park at Háls farm, find the marked trail and venture on a short and adventurous hike.

 Scan to find more things to do in Akureyri online

NORTH ICELAND

LEGENDS | HORSES | LANDSCAPES

Experience
North
Iceland
online

NORTH ICELAND
Trip Builder

■■■■ The region is characterised by dramatic and diverse landscapes, many lakes and rivers, powerful waterfalls, tall mountains, volcanoes and geothermal areas. There are also green pastures, free roaming sheep and horses, and diverse wildlife.

Grímsey

Head to **Grímsey** island, the northernmost part of Iceland (p191)
🕑 2 days

Flatey

Eyjafjörður
Ólafsfjörður

Join local food workshops at Brimslóð Atelier in **Blönduós** (p180)
🕑 ½–1 day

Skagafjörður

Learn the herring history of beautiful **Siglufjörður** (p187)
🕑 ½ day

Dalvík
Grenivík
Laufás

Sauðárkrókur

Húnafjörður

Tjörn

Reynisstaður

Myrkarjökull

Akureyri

Húnavellir

Varmahlíð

Háls

Hrafnagil

Learn about the last execution in Iceland at **Þrístapar** (p187)
🕑 ½ day

Go on epic horse treks and experience round-ups in **Skagafjörður** (p193)
🕑 1–8 days

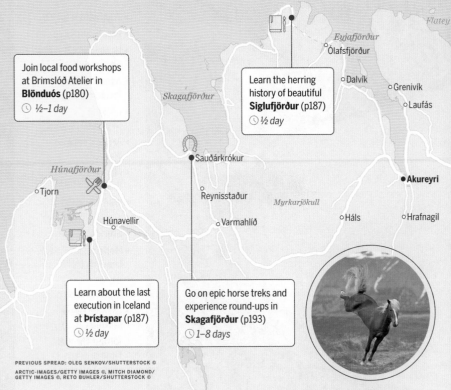

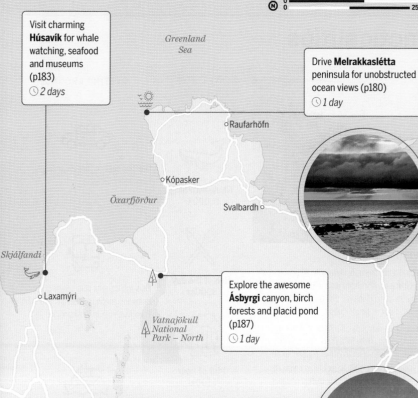

Visit charming **Húsavík** for whale watching, seafood and museums (p183)
🕓 2 days

Drive **Melrakkaslétta** peninsula for unobstructed ocean views (p180)
🕓 1 day

Explore the awesome **Ásbyrgi** canyon, birch forests and placid pond (p187)
🕓 1 day

Experience the magic of **Mývatn** in summer and winter (p196)
🕓 1–2 days

Tour the northern highlands to **Askja** caldera (p196)
🕓 1 day

Explore bookable experiences in North Iceland online

0   50 km
0   25 miles

Greenland Sea

○ Raufarhöfn

○ Kópasker

Öxarfjörður

Svalbardh ○

Skjálfandi

○ Laxamýri

Vatnajökull National Park – North

Reykjahlíð

Mývatn

Skútustaðir

Vatnajökull National Park

Egilsstaðir ●

Practicalities

TRUSOV/SHUTTERSTOCK ©

ARRIVING

Airports Flights from Reykjavík to Akureyri connect to Grímsey, Þórshöfn and Vopnafjörður, and from Reykjavík to Húsavík. For onward transport, hire a rental car or book taxis or shuttles.

Bus Strætó (straeto.is) offers tours from Reykjavík to Akureyri (Rte 57). From Akureyri there are infrequent services to other places. In small towns you might be able to get where you're going on foot. There are rarely buses or taxis.

HOW MUCH FOR A

Whale watching
11,000kr

Fish of the day
3900kr

Pint of beer
1300kr

GETTING AROUND

Car It's best to hire a car to get between places.

Bus Infrequent bus connections between main towns (straeto.is). Free public bus in Akureyri.

Ferry Scheduled ferry trips between Árskógssandur and Hrísey and Dalvík and Grímsey.

WHEN TO GO

JAN–MAR
Short days. Northern Lights. Possible snow, ice. Ski season.

APR–JUN
Midnight sun (late June). Migrating birds. Off-piste skiing.

JUL–SEP
Festival season. Highland roads open. Best for outdoor activities.

OCT–DEC
Colder, shorter days. Northern Lights. Autumn colours.

EATING & DRINKING

Icelandic Most restaurants in coastal towns serve local seafood. Try the catch of the day. Lamb is a must. They graze in mountain pastures in the summer and taste like game.

Skyr Buy this yoghurt-like dessert (pictured) in supermarkets or find it on menus in classic or creative combinations.

Cafes and bakeries Open early in the mornings and popular among locals. Try the *kleinur* (twisted doughnuts; pictured).

Best local seafood experiences Bounty of the Sea (p180)

Must-try beer bath Bjórböðin SPA (p197)

WHERE TO STAY

There are varied sleeping options throughout the region. It's best to book in advance.

CONNECT & FIND YOUR WAY

Wi-fi Free and available in most hotels, bars, restaurants and public buildings. There is GSM/3G/4G coverage everywhere except the remotest areas.

Navigation Ask for guidance at tourist information centres and hotels. Google Maps is helpful, but check online (vegagerdin.is) for road conditions and closures. Search online for other useful info (northiceland.is, safetravel.is).

Town	Pro/Con
Húnavatnssýslur / Húnaþing	Hvammstangi, Blönduós and Skagaströnd. Base for seal watching and horseback riding.
Skagafjörður	Sauðárkrókur, Varmahlíð, Hofsós and the Sturlunga Trail. Base for horseback riding and river rafting.
Fjallabyggð	Siglufjörður and Ólafsfjörður. Base for water sports, skiing and hiking.
Eyjafjörður	Dalvík, Akureyri, Hrísey and Grímsey. Base for skiing, hiking, boat tours, water sports, art and culture.
Suður-Þingeyjarsýsla & Norðurþing	Grenivík, Húsavík, Mývatn, volcanoes and geothermal areas. Base for whale and bird watching and highland tours.
Norður-Þingeyjarsýsla & Langanesbyggð	Ásbyrgi, Melrakkaslétta and Langanes. Base for nature exploration, birdwatching, slow travel and solitude.

DISCOUNT CARD

The Camping Card Provides access to several campgrounds around Iceland (maximum 28 nights for one family) for €159. Order online at campingcard.is.

MONEY

Cards are widely accepted and often preferred. Some tour operators and small-scale vendors ask for cash. Find ATMs in most towns.

26 HEAVENLY
Showstopper

STARGAZING | NORTHERN LIGHTS | MIDNIGHT SUN

▬▬▬ The sky above North Iceland puts on a show in all seasons. Here, on the edge of the Arctic Circle, the sun never sets in summer and hardly rises in winter. Dark, clear skies are sprinkled with millions of stars and, sometimes, the Northern Lights come out to dance.

MARTIN BARTUSEK/SHUTTERSTOCK ©

🗺 Trip Notes

Getting around Car is the best way to travel through North Iceland.

When to go Late August to early May for stargazing and Northern Lights. Mid-June to mid-July for midnight sun. Meteor showers in August and November.

Top tip Search online for info on Northern Lights and midnight sun: forecasts (auroraforecast.is), best locations (arcticcoastway.is), tours (northiceland.is).

🏛 Monument to the Dwarves

The **Arctic Henge** in Raufarhöfn is a monument made of four 6m-tall gates and one 10m column. The gates – called Austri, Norðri, Suðri and Vestri after the dwarves in Norse mythology that hold up the sky – function as sundials. Still under construction, the Arctic Henge will eventually be a monument to all 72 dwarves named in Eddic poem *Völuspá*.

02 On the western Skagi Peninsula off Rd 745 is the cove **Kálfshamarsvík** with spectacular columnar basalt formations and a lighthouse. Wonderful place to enjoy the midnight sun or the Northern Lights.

04 On the eastern end of the **Múlagöng** tunnel by Ólafsfjörður is a rest area facing north with a view of Grímsey island. Excellent spot for stars, Northern Lights and midnight sun.

03 A sculpture of ferryman Jón Ósmann stands on the beach **Furðustrandir** near Sauðárkrókur. The ferryman is happy to pose against glowing sunsets and sparkling skies.

05 Hike up 417m **Húsavíkurfjall**. The mountain overlooks Húsavík and Skjálfandi bay, as well as Flatey and Lundey, and is great for viewing celestial shows.

01 Take Rd 711 to **Borgarvirki**, a 177m-high volcanic plug used as a fortress during the Saga Age. It has a viewing dial inside and offers a splendid view of Húnaflói bay. It's a great place for enjoying the midnight sun.

Map labels:

Flatey
Siglufjörður
Skjálfandi
Húsavík
Hraun
Skagafjörður
Ólafsfjörður
Eyjafjörður
Í Fjörðum
Laxamýri
Málmey
Dalvík
Skagheiði
Grenivík
Hofsós
Tröllaskagi Peninsula
Laufás
Skagaströnd
Viðvík
Hólar
Akureyri
Sauðárkrókur
Hofstaðir
Myrkjárjökull
Húnafjörður
Blönduós
Háls
Þristapar
Hof

Astronomical
ICELAND

01 Aurora borealis

The mesmerising Northern Lights appear due to disturbances in the magnetosphere caused by solar wind. Tiny particles enter the atmosphere and collide with molecules, making them glow.

02 Meteor showers

Celestial events in which myriad radiating meteors appear to fly at high speed from one point in the sky. The Perseids arrive in August and the Leonids in November.

03 Ursa Major

Or 'Great Bear' is a constellation known from the asterism of its main seven stars. It's visible from the northern hemisphere and goes by many other names (Karlsvagninn in Icelandic).

04 Cassiopeia

The constellation can be seen by the naked eye from a northern location. Its five brightest stars – Alpha, Beta, Gamma, Delta and Epsilon – create the easily recognisable 'W' shape.

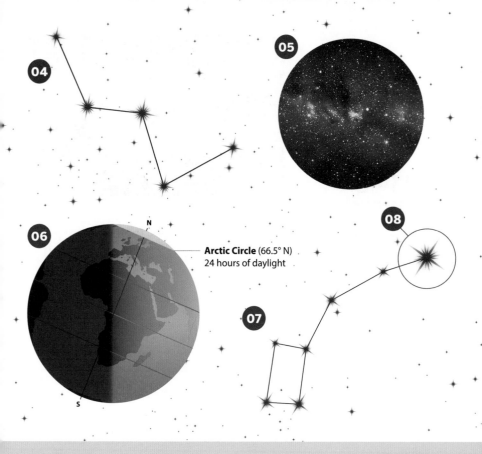

Arctic Circle (66.5° N)
24 hours of daylight

N

S

05 Milky Way

The galaxy that contains our solar system appears as a hazy band of light stretching across the winter sky from the east to the west. It's known as Vetrarbrautin (Winter Path) in Icelandic.

06 Midnight sun

At summer solstice (around June 21) – when the earth has its maximum axial tilt towards the sun – there is no sunrise or sunset at Iceland's most northerly point, Grímsey island.

07 Ursa Minor

Or 'Little Bear' is another constellation of seven stars, which also resembles a ladle. The constellation was important for navigators because it includes the Pole Star.

08 Pole Star

Also known as Polaris or North Star, the Pole Star is a very bright triple star system. It lies nearly in a direct line with the Earth's rotational axis 'above' the North Pole and appears to stand still.

MAGNIFIER/SHUTTERSTOCK ©

Looking Skyward

CELESTIAL PHENOMENA ABOVE ICELAND

The Northern Lights are an obvious attraction for visitors to Iceland during the dark season. However, if the aurora borealis won't put on a show during your stay, direct your attention towards the twinkling stars.

'As soon as you get out of the light pollution you can find good conditions for stargazing. The constellation Cassiopeia is easy to find in the evening. Right above your head you'll see a 'W'. Ursa Major can easily be identified by its characteristic ladle shape, and it points towards Ursa Minor and Pole Star', says Valdís Björk Þorsteinsdóttir, chair of the Stjörnu-Oddi stargazing society.

'At certain times of the year it's almost guaranteed that you can see meteor showers. The Perseids are always in August and the Leonids in November. They're named after the constellations from which they seem to appear', she explains. 'You can also see the glow of the Milky Way, which extends from the east to the west. It's like a brighter stripe or lustre across the sky.'

Although the lunar eclipses in 2022 will not be clearly visible from North Iceland, Valdís says that the moon is always an interesting sight. 'In the summer you can see amazing sunsets. When the midnight sun is shining you don't see much else, but it brings on its own show in the evening.'

Medieval Astronomer

Oddi Helgason, or Stjörnu-Oddi, was an Icelandic astronomer who worked as a farmhand at Múli in Aðaldalur in the 12th century. His observations of the summer solstice, the weekly change of the sun's declination and the varying arrival of twilight in North Iceland proved important for timekeeping and navigation. They were Iceland's most valuable contribution to natural sciences in the Middle Ages. Seafarers used the position of the sun to estimate their course, as well as the Pole Star after dark.

Left Milky Way above Goðafoss **Middle** Northern Lights **Right** Star trails moving around the Pole Star

'It's incredible that Stjörnu-Oddi was given the scope to make these observations', says Valdís, whose society is named after the medieval astronomer. 'He timed the spring equinox much more accurately than others had done. He measured the diameter of the sun as a ratio of the entire arc across the sky. It's much more accurate than the church's official number at that time', she states. 'He used a method where he noted where the sunray hit the wall through a small crack on the door and made his calculations that way.'

> At certain times of the year it's almost guaranteed that you can see meteor showers.

Not much is known about Stjörnu-Oddi or his methods, but he was likely self-educated and had no books to reference – he may even have been illiterate. He is known to have spent time on Flatey island where there is a mysterious circular construction called Arnargerði. Some believe that it served as an astronomical observatory that Stjörnu-Oddi used for his studies. A memorial to Stjörnu-Oddi was unveiled at Grenjaðarstaður, a turf farm and museum in Aðaldalur, at the summer solstice on 20 June 2020.

📖 Celestial Phenomena in Norse Mythology

Stars The sparks that flew from Múspellsheimur – the burning hot world in Norse mythology – as stated in *Snorra-Edda*'s description of the creation of the world.

Sun and Moon The siblings Sól and Máni. Sól drives the sun's carriage across the sky and Máni leads the moon on its path. Both the sun and moon are being chased by wolves, which is why they are constantly on the move. At Ragnarök – doomsday – wolves will swallow the heavenly bodies, blacken the sun and turn the sky blood red.

Bifröst The bridge between heaven and earth, which connects the world of gods, Ásgarður, with the world of men, Miðgaður. In *Snorra-Edda* it is stated that Bifröst is the rainbow, although it has also been described as the Northern Lights or the Milky Way.

27 ARCTIC
Coast Way

SEAFOOD | BEACHES | SLOW TRAVEL

▬▬▬ Take your time when driving the Arctic Coast Way. It's close to the Ring Rd yet it feels far from the beaten track. It takes you between desolate places where time seems to slow down, where people live off the sea and their lives are dictated by the whims of the weather.

LARIGAN · PATRICIA HAMILTON/
GETTY IMAGES ©

🗺 Trip Notes

Getting around Hire a car at Keflavík International Airport when you arrive in the country. Make sure it's fit for gravel roads.

When to go Best driving conditions are in summer. Not all roads are cleared in winter, but there are alternative routes (arcticcoastway.is). September to May for Northern Lights; mid-June to mid-July for midnight sun.

Top tip For solitude, the westernmost and easternmost parts of the Arctic Coast Way are your best bet.

🐟 Bounty of the Sea

Dive into local culture and history through 'hero' experiences (arcticcoastway.is). **Brimslóð Atelier** in Blönduós offers workshops on local seafood, wild herbs and other raw ingredients. The **Herring Era Museum** in Siglufjörður takes visitors back to the herring boom. In Hauganes, catch your own fish, learn about salt fish and enjoy a meal at **Baccalá Bar**.

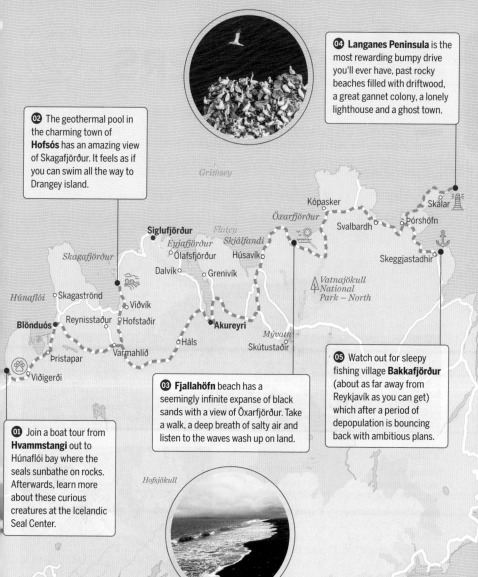

04 **Langanes Peninsula** is the most rewarding bumpy drive you'll ever have, past rocky beaches filled with driftwood, a great gannet colony, a lonely lighthouse and a ghost town.

02 The geothermal pool in the charming town of **Hofsós** has an amazing view of Skagafjörður. It feels as if you can swim all the way to Drangey island.

Grímsey

Kópasker

Öxarfjörður

Skálar

Siglufjörður   *Flatey*   Svalbardh   Þórshöfn

Eyjafjörður   *Skjálfandi*

○Ólafsfjörður   Húsavík○

Skagafjörður   Dalvík○   Skeggjastadhir

○Grenivík

Húnaflói   ○Skagaströnd   △Vatnajökull
                                              National
                                              Park – North

                ○Viðvík

Blönduós●   Reynisstaður ○Hofstaðir   ●**Akureyri**

                                Mývatn

                ○Háls   Skútustaðir○

         ○Þristapar   Varmahlíð

○Viðigerði

05 Watch out for sleepy fishing village **Bakkafjörður** (about as far away from Reykjavík as you can get) which after a period of depopulation is bouncing back with ambitious plans.

03 **Fjallahöfn** beach has a seemingly infinite expanse of black sands with a view of Öxarfjörður. Take a walk, a deep breath of salty air and listen to the waves wash up on land.

01 Join a boat tour from **Hvammstangi** out to Húnaflói bay where the seals sunbathe on rocks. Afterwards, learn more about these curious creatures at the Icelandic Seal Center.

Hofsjökull

0 ——— 50 km
0 ——— 25 miles

28 Flippers & FEATHERS

SAIL | WALK | WILDLIFE

▬ Northeast Iceland is home to Iceland's whale-watching capital and a prime location for birdwatching. There are puffins, of course, but also many more species worthy of attention, including harlequin ducks, gyrfalcons and northern gannets.

S.T HORS/SHUTTERSTOCK ©

🗺 How to

Getting there Hire a car on arrival at Keflavík International Airport. Or fly from Reykjavík to either Akureyri or Húsavík. Once in the north, a car is the most practical means of transport.

When to go Summer is peak season for watching whales and birds.

Tour operators Regional tour operators listed online (northiceland.is).

Expect to pay Guided two- to three-hour whale-watching tours adult/child from 10,500/4000kr.

ADRIAN EUGEN CIOBANIUC/SHUTTERSTOCK ©

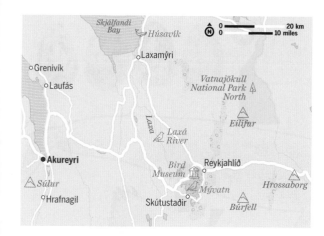

Whale-Watching Capital

A town of 2300 people, **Húsavík** stands by Skjálfandi bay where 11 species of whales and dolphins can be sighted. Humpbacks are the most common species, but the elusive blue whale, the world's largest animal, sometimes makes an appearance. Normally, about 1000 people a day go whale watching with Húsavík's four whale-watching companies from April to October. The University of Iceland has a **research centre** on marine biology in town and the **Húsavík Whale Museum**, with its massive blue-whale skeleton, teaches visitors about these fascinating creatures. **Geosea Geothermal Sea Baths** has a view of Skjálfandi, and sometimes whales can be seen from there.

Birds of Paradise

A paradise for bird lovers, lake **Mývatn** hosts 14 species of nesting ducks – such as tufted duck, greater scaup, Eurasian wigeon and common scoter – which is unique in the northern hemisphere. The banks of **Laxá** river are the prime habitat for harlequin ducks and Barrow's goldeneye in Iceland. Also watch out for gyrfalcons on the hunt. Find Sigurgeir's **Bird Museum** in a beautiful building by the lake. On display are 280 taxidermic birds – nearly every species that nests in Iceland – and 300 eggs.

Top Humpback whale breaches near Húsavík **Bottom** Tufted duck

🦆 Birding Trail

Birdwatching enthusiasts should venture along the **Birding Trail of Northeast Iceland** (birdingtrail. is), which connects places known for their rich and varied birdlife, such as wetlands, rivers, lakes and ponds, sea cliffs and coastal areas, heaths and highlands. Myriad bird species can be seen on the trail: seabirds, waterfowl, waders, passerines, ducks and raptors.

WILD
Things

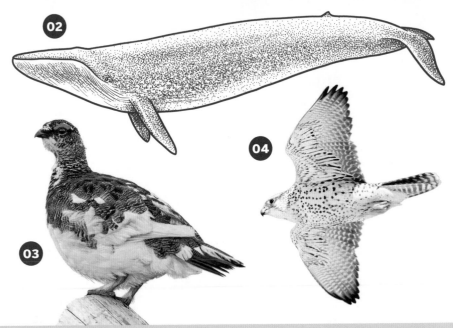

01 Bird eggs

The eggs of guillemots and other seabirds are collected from cliffs on Grímsey island. While an acquired taste, they're definitely eye candy. Arctic Trip offers egg-collecting tours.

02 Blue whale

The largest animal this world has ever seen, the blue whale can sometimes be sighted on whale-watching tours in North Iceland.

03 Ptarmigan

This bird has feathered claws and changes colour three times a year to blend in with the environment and hide from predators.

04 Gyrfalcon

One of the gyrfalcon's prime habitats is the Jökulsárgljúfur canyons. The Falcon Centre is located in Ásbyrgi.

05 Humpback whale

Commonly sighted on whale-watching tours, humpbacks can be identified by the pattern on their flukes. They migrate some 25,000km each year, further than any other mammal.

06 Northern gannet

A large and elegant migratory seabird known for its high-speed dives into the sea. There are large gannet on Melrakkaslétta and on Langanes.

07 Arctic tern

Migrates further than any other bird on the planet, from the high Arctic to Antarctica. It nests by the coast, lakes and wetlands.

08 Orca

The world's largest dolphin species. These highly intelligent creatures hunt in groups and develop different techniques for different areas.

09 Harlequin duck

This colourful bird is found in fast-flowing streams in Northeast Iceland year-round, primarily in Laxá river near Mývatn.

29 Journey Through **STORIES**

FOLKLORE | FILM | HISTORY

▬▬ Visit places steeped in history, tour museums celebrating tradition and participate in interactive exhibitions and events that take you back in time. Stories, old and new, add another dimension to your journey.

STEPHAN LANGHANS/SHUTTERSTOCK ©

🗺 **How to**

Getting around Hire a car and DIY or book sight-seeing tours for specific experiences.

When to go Year-round, but most events take place in summer.

Top tip The local tourist information centres can help you plan your trip, as can online resources (northiceland.is, saga-trail.is).

FOTOVOYAGER/GETTY IMAGES ©

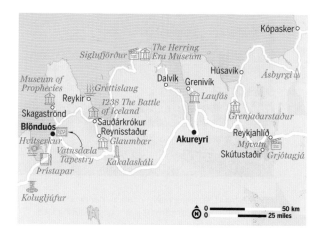

Myths and legends These are often interwoven with nature and landscape. Sea stack **Hvítserkur** was a troll that turned to stone; the falls in **Kolugljúfur** are named after the ogress who lived in the gorge; and the horseshoe-shaped canyon **Ásbyrgi** was created when Sleipnir, Norse god Óðinn's eight-legged horse, stepped down from heaven.

Submerge in the sagas Bathe in **Grettislaug** where Grettir the Strong warmed up after his swim from Drangey island. Visit the **Museum of Prophecies** in Skagaströnd, dedicated to settler Þórdís the Prophetess, and in Blönduós, help stitch the **Vatnsdæla Tapestry**, documenting the *Vatnsdæla Saga*.

Sturlunga Trail This trail in Skagafjörður connects places significant to the bloodiest period in Iceland's history, which led to the end of the commonwealth era. At **Kakalaskáli** find a monument and exhibition about the battle of Haugsnesbardagi in 1246, and in **1238 – The Battle of Iceland** you can become a warrior through virtual reality.

Turf farms These kept Icelanders warm and safe for centuries. **Glaumbær**, **Laufás** and **Grenjaðarstaður** are preserved as living museums, where you can step into history and experience traditional country life, haymaking and folk dancing.

Film and literature Visit **Þrístapar** and other sites connected with the last execution in Iceland in 1830, made famous in Hannah Kent's *Burial Rites*. Near **Mývatn** is Grjótagjá, the water-filled cave where Jon Snow and Ygritte from *Game of Thrones* had a steamy soak. Crime series *Trapped* was filmed in **Siglufjörður**.

Top Ásbyrgi canyon **Bottom** Hvítserkur sea stack

Living History

The Herring Era Museum

Provides insight into the Siglufjörður's herring boom in the mid-20th century. In the summer, the atmosphere is recreated with salting exhibitions at the pier with 'herring girls' salting herring in barrels to live accordion music.

Medieval Days

This brings the ancient trading centre Gásir back to life in late July. Watch a blacksmith beat metal, women dye wool with herbs and bake bread over an open fire. Also test your sharpshooting skills with a bow and arrow and help egg a thief.

CANDASTOCK/SHUTTERSTOCK ©

Modern Legends

QUIRKY TOWNS AND ALIEN ATMOSPHERE

Not only do Icelandic landscapes feature in medieval sagas and folk stories passed orally from generation to generation but also in modern murder mysteries, fantasy and sci-fi movies. Iceland has grown in popularity as a filming location and the North plays a big part.

Þór Kjartansson, supervising location manager at True North production company, is ever busy scouting locations for filmmakers from around the world. 'It's often a long process, especially with larger movies.' He explains that it takes a lot of back and forth before the right place is found. It needs to fulfil certain conditions, for example, be near the sea but not too remote and face the sun. 'The camera crews always fall for the light. They hate blue sky and sunlight – but that is rarely the condition in Iceland.'

Out of This World

Fast & Furious 8, which included a car race on lake Mývatn, is among Þór's most memorable projects. 'It was amazing to be able to carry out a Hollywood scene of that scale on the frozen lake.' The landscape scenes for *Star Wars: The Mandalorian* at the site of the 2014–15 Holuhraun eruption in the northern highlands also stand out. 'It was a unique experience because it was so difficult to access and film the barren landscape all around the lava, the desert and untouched wilderness north of Vatnajökull glacier.' *Rogue One: A Star Wars Story* was filmed in various locations in Iceland, including the Krafla geothermal area near Mývatn. 'We shot scenes around Leirhnjúkur mountain in the snow', reveals Þór.

North Icelandic nature represents another planet in Ridley Scott's *Prometheus*. In the opening scene an extraterrestrial drinks a deadly potion and tumbles into a massive waterfall – Dettifoss. In post-apocalyptic *Oblivion*, ancient crater Hrossaborg serves as a devastated football stadium. In 2020, scenes for a TV series starring Will Smith were shot at Jökulsárgljúfur canyon in Vatnajökull National Park.

Left Boats moored at Húsavík **Middle** Dettifoss **Right** Holuhraun eruption

Eurovision Town

Eurovision Song Contest: The Story of Fire Saga with Will Ferrell is of a totally different genre. 'The producers were looking for an Icelandic town to set the story in', says Þór. True North's first suggestion was Stykkishólmur and the producers loved it, but after they visited Húsavík, there was no turning back. 'Húsavík kind of stole the show', laughs Þór. In the comedy, main character Lars stubbornly pursues his dream of competing in the Eurovision Song Contest instead of becoming a fisherman like his father. At the 2021 Academy Awards, Húsavík stole the show again: the film's title song was nominated for an Oscar and True North recorded a music video with singer Molly Sandén and a local girl choir in Húsavík.

> The region is so diverse, not only because of the varied landscapes but because they change from season to season.

'In North Iceland you find these special forces of nature in the shape of glaciers and lava, desert sands, canyons and waterfalls, from Kverkfjöll mountains to Dettifoss and Mývatn', states Þór. 'The region is so diverse, not only because of the varied landscapes but because they change from season to season. You can shoot at almost exactly the same location in summer, winter, autumn and spring and it looks totally different because of the changing light and colours, and whether it's covered in snow or not.'

🎬 North Iceland in Icelandic Films

The Last Fishing Trip (*Síðasta veiðiferðin*; 2020) A comedy about middle-aged friends who go fishing – and everything goes wrong! It was shot at Mýrarkvísl river.

The Swan (*Svanurinn*; 2017) The story of a nine-year-old girl who is sent away to live at a farm and gets caught up in dramatic events. The film was shot in Svarfaðardalur valley.

Rams (*Hrútar*; 2015) Features two brothers who haven't spoken in 40 years despite living next to each other on sheep farms in Bárðardalur valley. When disaster strikes, they must stick together.

30 ISLAND
Explorations

BIRDS | FISH | PEOPLE

The islands off North Iceland are a world of their own. In the past the communities had to be self-sufficient to survive when stormy weather cut off all connection with the mainland. This isolation still marks the island communities, with people attracted by the prospect of winding down off the grid.

📷 How to

Getting there Ferries go to Hrísey from Árskógssandur and to Grímsey from Dalvík. Planes fly to Grímsey from Akureyri, but tours are required for Drangey and Flatey.

When to go Year-round for Hrísey and Grímsey. Summer for Drangey and Flatey. October to March for birdwatching.

Top tip For info on the islands and tours, check online (northiceland.is, arcticcoastway.is).

Doppelganger Don't confuse North Iceland's Flatey with the island of the same name in the Westfjords.

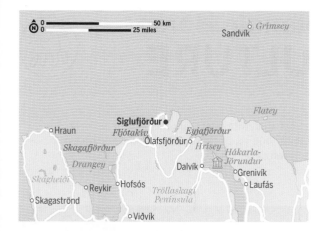

Drangey This 180m rock used to be Skagafjörður's 'food chest'. It's home to myriad birds but no people (although Grettir 'the strong' lived there as an outlaw). Farmers rowed over with their sheep for grazing, hunted birds and collected eggs. The panoramic view of the fjord is worth the climb. Guided tours offered May to August.

Hrísey Has 160 residents, many of whom live off the sea, as their ancestors did. The museum of **Hákarla-Jörundur** tells the story of shark fishing; shark oil was used for street lighting in Europe. The island is known for its rich birdlife and is a sanctuary for ptarmigans. Wild angelica is harvested for supplement production. Old tractors are used for transport rather than cars. Locals take it slow and are applying to become a Cittaslow community. The ferry goes from Árskógssandur year-round in only 15 minutes.

Grímsey The only place in Iceland that stretches across the Arctic Circle. The 60 residents live off fishing and increasingly tourism. People visit for the myriad puffins and other seabirds and quiet walks among friendly sheep. It's possible to snorkel or dive with the birds, collect guillemot eggs (a local delicacy) from cliffs, and go on fishing tours. It's connected by ferry to Dalvík and by air to Akureyri.

Flatey It used to be a thriving community, but in 1967 all residents packed their things and left. The houses stood empty until the islanders' relatives and Húsavík locals saved them from decay. The island is now their private paradise, where they can get away from the hustle and bustle of daily life.

Top Drangey **Bottom** Tractor 'taxi' on Hrísey

⚜ Island Festivals

Sólstöðuhátíð
Grímsey locals invite visitors to join them for a celebration of the summer solstice around 21 June each year. Enjoy fresh seafood, listen to live music, go sailing and watch the sun not set.

Hríseyjarhátíð
The Hrísey family festival is held annually in July. Locals invite visitors to come and enjoy coffee in their gardens, offer beach walks, tractor tours, games and entertainment for kids, traditional dances, live music and a singalong by the bonfire. Many choose to camp. (visitakureyri.is)

31 Icelandic Horse
CULTURE

RIDING | FAMILY | NATURE

■■■ You will never feel closer to nature than from the back of an Icelandic horse. Pure-bred for more than 1000 years, these soft-gaited creatures carry travellers across streams and rough terrain.

ARCTIC-IMAGES/GETTY IMAGES ©

🗺 How to

Getting here Hire a car at Keflavík International Airport, or fly from Reykjavík to Akureyri or Húsavík. A car is your best bet for getting around.

When to go Most tours are in summer. Early summer for newborn foals; autumn for horse round-ups.

Tour operators Many companies offer horse-related experiences (see northiceland.is).

What to wear Warm, waterproof and comfortable clothing. For longer tours, proper riding clothing, sunscreen and lip balm.

IMAGEBROKER/REINHARD PANTKE/GETTY IMAGES ©

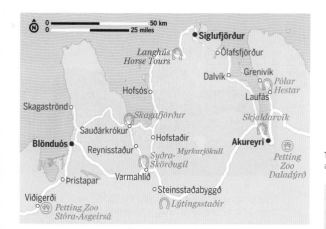

Top Icelandic horses **Bottom** Horses and riders on frozen lake Mývatn

Choose Your Experience

Family-friendly Petting zoos include **Daladýrð** and **Stóra-Ásgeirsá**. **Lýtingsstaðir** and **Langhús Horse Tours** offer special experiences for children too young for tours. Many horse farms have accommodation or are open for drop-ins.

Shorter excursions If you're new to horses or don't ride regularly, book shorter excursions, for example at the aforementioned farms or at **Skjaldarvík**, **Pólar hestar** and **Syðra-Skörðugil**. Tours are guided and often include storytelling; the experience varies depending on the season and surrounding landscape. Riding gear and safety equipment is included.

Multi-day tours Experience the freedom of riding for days through wild nature or highland landscapes, along ancient routes and narrow sheep paths in a smooth *tölt* (running walk) pace or galloping with a herd of loose horses. These tours are magic but are only for experienced riders. Operators include **Íslandshestar** and **Riding Iceland**. Midnight-sun tours, Diamond Circle tours and round-up tours are among the experiences on offer.

Skagafjörður This region is the centre of Icelandic horsemanship with many of the best-known breeding farms and horse roundups. Hólar University – which teaches equine science, among other subjects – is located there, as well as the Icelandic Horse History Centre (open in summer and by appointment). Landsmót, the National Icelandic Horse Competition, will be held at Hólar in 2026.

🐎 Horse Festivals

Stóðréttir
These horse round-ups are true country festivals when farmers round up their horses from summer pastures in the mountains. Watch hundreds of horses being herded and sorted in a paddock called a *rétt*. There are food and local handicrafts for sale, and singing and dancing in the evening. Three of the best-known round-ups are **Laufskálarétt**, **Víðidalstungurétt** and **Skrapatungurétt**, held in late September, early October (check bbl.is).

Horses on Ice – Mývatn Open
An annual riding competition on the frozen lake Mývatn in mid-March. Watch superb horses and riders 'fly' across the ice. **Saltvík** gives visitors the chance to ride on ice. (visitmyvatn.is)

Tölting Through Time

FROM MOST INDISPENSABLE SERVANT TO MOST LOYAL COMPANION

When settlers arrived in Iceland in the 9th century CE, they brought domestic animals, including horses of different breeds, which became the ancestors of the Icelandic horse.

SASCHA KILMER/GETTY IMAGES ©

'The land has shaped this breed for 1000 years', says Jelena Ohm, project manager for Horses of Iceland, the official marketing initiative for the Icelandic horse. The small and sturdy breed was used for transport and farm work. It developed a double coat to keep warm in winter. Today still, horses are kept outside except when they are being trained for riding, and in the summer large herds roam free in mountain valleys. 'They have a very strong connection with nature', says Jelena. 'Because they grow up in a natural environment, they are very smart and learn quickly, which makes them very fun to ride and train.' Due to better feed and selective breeding the horse has grown taller over recent decades.

Five Different Gaits

The Icelandic horse has two extra gaits in addition to walk, trot and canter: The soft *tölt* for the comfort of riders, and the super smooth and fast flying pace for racing short distances. Other horse breeds have, or used to have, similar gaits. However, while in Europe there were roads and horses pulled carriages, in Iceland there were none and people rode their horses across rough terrain. Therefore, the *tölt* maintained its importance. 'What is special about the Icelandic horse is that it's one of the few breeds where all five gaits are trained and competed in', states Jelena. 'With the industrial revolution, roads and cars, the horse's role changed from being "the most indispensable servant", to a competition and hobby horse, and it's still a big part of today's culture.'

Left Icelandic horses graze near lake Mývatn **Middle** Riders explore Iceland's landscapes **Right** Man with Icelandic horse

Passion for the Horse

Horses are unusually common in Iceland. A 2019 report revealed that in Iceland there are 240 horses per 1000 inhabitants, while in Sweden, which has the highest ratio in the EU, it's 32 horses per 1000 inhabitants. The horses are also popular among travellers. From 2014 to 2018 the number of visitors enjoying horse-related tourism jumped from 120,000 to 287,000, and a 2018 survey on horse treks found that nine out of 10 tourists loved the experience.

> Because they grow up in a natural environment, they are very smart and learn quickly, which makes them very fun to ride and train.

Horse Legends

Sleipnir Óðinn's eight-legged horse is the most famous horse in Norse mythology. But there are many other mythological horses, including **Skinfaxi**, which Dagur (Day) rides across the sky; and **Hrímfaxi**, which is ridden by his mother Nótt (Night).

Fluga One of the four-legged settlers named in the *Book of Settlement* (Landnáma). The famous horse-breeding farm Flugumýri in Skagafjörður – which is also the site of the fateful arson in the *Sturlunga Saga* – was named after the mare.

Faxi An important character in the ghost story *Djákninn á Myrká* (The Deacon of Dark River). Faxi's rider, the deacon, died when Faxi fell through the ice on a river they were crossing. The deacon came back to haunt his fiancé and took her for a ride on Faxi in the moonlight.

🎬 In Film & Literature

Of Horses and Men (*Hross í oss*; 2013) A multi-awarded country romance by Benedikt Erlingsson, seen from the perspective of horses.

Nonni and Manni (*Nonni und Manni*; 1988-89) A children's TV series based on the books of Icelandic author Nonni (Jón Sveinsson). In one scene, Nonni's horse saves his life.

Skúlaskeið This poem by Grímur Thomsen celebrates Sörli, the horse that saved its owner Skúli, a murder convict, by pacing across rocky terrain in Kaldidalur, outrunning everyone and bringing Skúli home – then died from exhaustion.

Listings

BEST OF THE REST

🌋 Volcanoes, Lava & Geothermal Areas

Krafla

The last series of eruptions in the Krafla volcanic system occurred from 1975 to 1984. A colourful and steaming world of wonder with turquoise crater lake Víti, the area makes for an otherworldly hike, only 30 minutes from lake Mývatn.

Þeistareykir

These geothermal fields are as colourful and steamy as Hverir (Námafjall) by Mývatn but less frequented. The power station built there in 2017 can be reached on paved road from Húsavík. You'll find various kinds of hot springs, mud pools and fumaroles.

Mývatn Area

All around lake Mývatn are spectacular craters and lava formations. **Dimmuborgir** are dark and eerie lava fields. Lava paths lead past fascinating structures like **Kirkjan** (the Church), a lava tube. **Hverfjall** is an easily accessible ancient crater.

Lofthellir

This permafrost lava tube can only be explored with a guide (GEO Travel offers guided tours year-round). It's not suitable for young children or those with claustrophobia because the opening is extremely narrow. Inside is a magical world of ice sculptures, frozen in time.

🏔 Highland Destinations

The following areas are only accessible in 4WD vehicles in summer, and tours are usually recommended.

Askja

This complex of calderas is surrounded by the Dyngjufjöll mountains. In the 1960s, the Apollo astronauts trained here for lunar missions. Other areas nearby include Drekagil canyon, Holuhraun (created in the 2014–15 eruption) and the green area of Herðubreiðalindir.

Kverkfjöll

On the northeastern border of Vatnajökull glacier lies the Kverkfjöll mountain range, made up of active volcanoes in one of the country's most powerful high-temperature geothermal areas. Go there for hiking and glacial exploration tours. Accommodation can be booked in Sigurðarskáli.

Hveravellir

Situated between glaciers Langjökull and Hofsjökull, Hveravellir Nature Reserve is a geothermal oasis on the highland route of Kjölur. It has a service centre, a campground, indoor accommodation, hiking trails and a natural pool. Drive there in a 4WD SUV in the summer or take the SBA bus.

Hveravellir

Laugarfell

Off the highland route across Sprengisandur lies Laugarfell, an oasis in the desert between Hofsjökull and Vatnajökull. The area has mountain huts open in summer, a natural geothermal pool for bathing and bubbling hot springs.

 ## Wondrous Waterfalls

Kolufoss

Kolugljúfur canyon with stunning Kolufoss is one of Northwest Iceland's most popular destinations, and a viewing platform was recently built there. The falls are in Víðidalur valley, a five-minute drive from the Ring Rd.

Reykjafoss

This beautiful waterfall in Skagafjörður is relatively unknown, perhaps because it is hidden from view until you're standing right next to it. At Vindheimamelar about 7km from Varmahlíð, there's a small parking area by the walking path that leads to the fall.

Falls in Skjálfandafljót

Goðafoss is right on the Ring Rd. An even more picturesque waterfall in glacial river Skjálfandafljót is **Aldeyjarfoss**, framed by columnar basalt. In summer it can be reached in regular cars by Rd 842 through Bárðardalur.

Falls in Jökulsá á Fjöllum

Dettifoss is the most powerful waterfall in Europe and one of the highlights of the Diamond Circle. Further upstream is the prettier **Selfoss**. For a complete series of falls, walk to **Hafragilsfoss**, too. A path leads between the three waterfalls.

 ## Baths & Beer

Beer Spa

Bathe in beer at Bjórböðin SPA in Árskógssandur while enjoying a Kaldi beer from tap – an experience brought to you by Iceland's oldest microbrewery, Bruggsmiðjan. There's

Kverkfjöll

also a hot tub with a view of Hrísey island. The restaurant serves dishes from local meat and fish – and beer. Complete your trip with a brewery tour.

'Forest Baths'

In a forest opposite Akureyri, new baths are under construction, set to open in February 2022. Hot water discovered while making the Vaðlaheiði tunnel will be channelled to the baths. Bathers can swim among the trees and have local draught beer at the swim-in bar.

GeoSea Geothermal Sea Baths

The wondrous infinity pools in Húsavík offer a magnificent view of Skjálfandi bay. The water contains mineral-rich seawater known to be good for the skin. For a more sublime experience still, try the locally brewed Húsavík Ale during your soak.

 ## River Rafting

Viking Rafting & Bakkaflöt

These operators offer rafting tours on the glacial rivers of Skagafjörður, mellower for families and more extreme for adventurous types. There's also white-water kayaking.

 Scan to find more things to do in North Iceland online

NORTH ICELAND REVIEWS

THE
WESTFJORDS

REMOTE | NATURE | ADVENTURE

Experience
the
Westfjords
online

THE WESTFJORDS
Trip Builder

Outdoor enthusiasts are spoilt for choice, so allow enough time to truly take in the region. Roads in the remote Westfjords can be windy, bumpy and slow, but for many this is half the attraction. The new tunnel between Arnarfjörður and Dýrafjörður has improved access, and other roadwork is underway.

Challenge yourself with an adventure activity tour around **Ísafjörður** (p211)
⏱ ½–6 days

Hornstrandir Nature Reserve
Hesteyri

Jökulfirðir
Grunnavík

Bolungarvík

Suðureyri ⚓

• Ísafjörður

Suðavík

Litlibær

Join a seafood-themed walking tour through **Suðureyri** fishing village (p212)
⏱ 2 hours

Svalvogar Núpur

Þingeyri

Marvel at **Dynjandi**, the region's largest waterfall (p209)
⏱ 1 hour

Observe puffins and other seabirds at one of Europe's largest bird cliffs, **Látrabjarg** (p209)
⏱ 1 hour

Arnarfjörður

Grænahlíð Hrafnseyri

Bildudalur

Patreksfjörður

Hnjótur

Foss

Flókalundur

Krossholt

Hvallátur

Vatnsfjörður Nature Reserve

Breiðafjörður

Walk remote golden-red **Rauðasandur** beach (p208)
⏱ 2+ hours

Immerse yourself in the natural hot spring and pool in **Reykjafjörður** (p209)
⏱ 1 hour

Explore bookable experiences in the Westfjords online

PREVIOUS SPREAD: KRZYSZTOF BARANOWSKI/GETTY IMAGES ©

Practicalities

ARRIVING

Air Flights from Reykjavík to Ísafjörður, Bíldudalur and Gjögur take 40 minutes.

Car The drive from Reykjavík to Ísafjörður is around 450km. Travel via Hólmavík on the region's east coast for paved-only roads.

FIND YOUR WAY

There are tourist information centres at Patreksfjörður, Þingeyri, Bolungarvík and Ísafjörður. (westfjords.is)

MONEY

There are stunning natural hot springs that are free to visit, but some have donation boxes to fund maintenance, so bring coins.

WHERE TO STAY

Town	Pro/Con
Ísafjörður	Largest town. Good base for visiting the region's north.
Patreksfjörður	Good base for the southern Westfjords.
Þingeyri	Beautifully situated. Less services and accommodation options.
Hólmavík	Largest settlement in Strandir. Several guesthouses, Airbnb and cabins.

EATING & DRINKING

Farm and sea Fish and lamb dominate restaurant menus. Catch your own fish on a sea angling tour.

Beer Dokkan Brugghús (pictured) is in Ísafjörður.

Artful dining Flak is an art venue, pub and restaurant in Patreksfjörður.

Food souvenir Saltverk (p213; pictured), Norður Salt (p213)

Best Belgian waffles Simbahöllin (p214)

Must-try seafood restaurant Tjöruhúsið (p214)

GETTING AROUND

Car Driving is the best way to get around (road.is).

Bus Connections can be infrequent and seasonal (westfjords.is).

Cycling Search online (cyclingiceland.is), and check out *The Biking Book of Iceland – Westfjords* by Ómar Smári Kristinsson.

 NOV–MAR Northern Lights, snowy landscapes, ski season Dec-Apr.

 APR–MAY Cooler than summer, less visitors.

 JUN–AUG Midnight sun for long days exploring.

 SEP–OCT Autumn colours, Northern Lights, some hotels, services closed.

32 Westfjords on
WATER

ACTIVITIES | WILDLIFE | SEA

▬▬▬ In a region essentially made up of fjords, you're never far from the sea. It makes sense then to explore the Westfjords on water. Kayaking, wildlife and whale-watching boat tours, sailing, diving and snorkelling are among the possibilities.

ELLI THOR MAGNUSSON/GETTY IMAGES ©

🗺 How to

When to go May to September is best for most tours, but check with operators.

Getting there Tour departure points include Ísafjörður, Ögur, Hólmavík, Heydalur and Norðurfjörður.

Tour operators The following offer water-based activities, including kayaking, whale and wildlife watching, sea angling, snorkelling, diving and sailing: aurora-arktika. com, beffatours.is, borea. is, divewestfjords.is, heydalur.is, lakitours.com, ogurtravel.is, strandferdir. is, wa.is, westtours.com.

DANIEL WESTERN/SHUTTERSTOCK ©

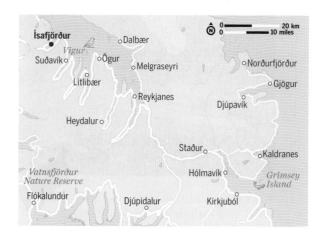

Top Woman kayaking, Westfjords
Bottom Sea urchin

Paddling paradise Meander the lengths of dramatic fjords and peninsulas for unforgettable panoramic views. On your journey you might encounter seals, seabirds, dolphins and even whales. Kayak out to the seabird colony of Vigur. Tours of different difficulty levels and lengths – from two hours to six days – are available.

Vintage Vigur Teeming with eider ducks, puffins and Arctic terns, the remote Vigur, situated in Ísafjarðardjúp, is a paradise for birdwatchers. The island (vigurisland.com) is inhabited year-round by just one family, who harvest the island's eiderdown, used for luxury bedding and clothing, and run the accommodation and cafe housed in a wooden house from 1860. There are just two rooms with kitchen for self-catering and limited small-group camping with basic facilities, so this place doesn't get too crowded. Overnight stays certainly aren't cheap – especially for camping – but do include pick up and drop off to this unique location.

Watching wildlife A range of whale species, including magnificent humpbacks, can be found in these waters. Whale- and birdwatching tours – including puffin tours to Grímsey island in Steingrímsfjörður – are available. Sea angling with the option to have your catch cooked for you are also available.

Going under To immerse yourself in the location, snorkel or dive in the fjord for a truly unique perspective. Private tours and gourmet diving tours with beach barbecue are available.

🐟 Beneath the Surface

The water here is very clean. It's also colder year-round than in the rest of the country but there's also better visibility. It's rich in marine life, such as scallops, mussels, urchins, seals, diving birds (like guillemot and razorbill), coralline algae (often pink) and maerl. There are also kelp forests and whale bones on the ocean floor at a 19th-century Norwegian whaling site. It's a great place to dive.

Sveinbjörn Hjálmarsson
Sveinbjörn is a professional diver, dive instructor and guide, and the owner of Dive Westfjords. He dives year-round to hand-pick sea urchins, scallops and mahogany clams for Nora seafood company. @simbikafari

Westfjords Way of Life

FISHING CONTINUES TO DOMINATE LIFE IN RURAL VILLAGES

Iceland and fishing are inextricably linked and no more so than in the Westfjords. You see this all around: small boat harbours, seafood menus, fish drying racks, processing plants, open-sea fish farms, and even an old cemetery for French fishermen.

Left Old fishing boats, Patreksfjörður **Middle** Dried fish tails **Right** Fisher, Ósvör Maritime Museum

'When you travel to the Westfjords, you still really sense that it's bound to fisheries', says Dr Matthias Kokorsch, academic director of the Coastal Communities and Regional Development Master's program at the University Centre of the Westfjords.

The rich fishing grounds have sustained rural communities here throughout history, but they have experienced difficult times over the past 25 years. This is due to technical changes and the privatisation of fishing quotas, resulting in quotas being accumulated by larger companies in fewer communities offering fewer jobs. 'Over the years, villages have lost fishing quotas and processing centres have been moved, so jobs have been lost', explains Matthias. The winter of 2019 was particularly tough, he says. There were avalanches and road closures, making it impossible for goods to be transported out. Avalanches in the village of Flateyri in January 2020 destroyed much of the fishing fleet. 'It's a difficult place to run a business.'

Changing Demographics

Over the years, the Westfjords communities have seen a downward population trend. 'It's really difficult to get young people to move back, especially when most of the opportunities are in fishing', says Matthias. Having said that, he remains optimistic for the future. 'Some places are actually seeing an increase and innovative projects get realised. But I also think it's important to consider quality of life; this isn't just about counting heads.'

Only around 10% of tourists visit the Westfjords. 'It's so tempting to just follow the Ring Rd. To get here, you have to deliberately go out of your way and you need time. This

means that the area isn't affected by mass tourism', explains Matthias. Tourists also mainly visit in the summer.

Creative Solutions

Although the economy has yet to really diversify beyond fishing, a number of creative projects aim to attract visitors and new residents to the region. Among them are innovation programs, the international-al master's programs in coastal studies, co-working spaces, art residencies and tourism initiatives like Suðureyri's Seafood Trail. There's also sea-related innovation, such as Kerecis' tissue-transplant products made from fish skin. Aquaculture has also grown rapidly in recent years, with fish farms now in several places. It's a contentious area due to concerns about potential environmental impacts. 'Aquaculture is a delicate topic. We must consider the environment, of course. On the issue of jobs, it's important to remember that even though it might not seem like many, in a small place like this, it can make a big difference.'

> A number of creative projects aim to attract visitors and new residents to the region. Among them are... tourism initiatives like Suðureyri's Seafood Trail.

The state-run Regional Development Institute's Fragile Communities program is among the innovation grants being offered to boost rural regions and halt depopulation. 'It just takes time. Regional development doesn't usually work with quick fixes', Matthias observes.

🏛 Museums

Ósvör Maritime Museum, Bolungarvík

Replica of a 19th-century fishing station, salt hut, fish drying area and drying hut down on the shore. A traditional fishing rowboat is also on display, as is fishing gear. (@osvor_sjominjasafn)

Westfjords Heritage Museum, Ísafjörður

Located in a cluster of houses from the 18th century. Gives an insight into the rich history and culture of the area. (nedsti.is)

Icelandic Sea Monster Museum, Bíldudalur

Several species of sea monsters are said to have been spotted in Arnarfjörður over the years, including the dragon-like Merhorse, known to threaten fishers and their boats. Learn more through words, pictures and multimedia displays. (skrimsli.is)

33 Road Trip
HIGHLIGHTS

LANDSCAPES | HIKING | POOLS

▬▬▬ The Westfjords Way (Vestfjarðaleiðin) scenic circular driving route takes you through the best of the Westfjords, including dramatic landscapes, natural hot springs and swimming pools. Launched in October 2020 with the opening of the tunnel between Arnarfjörður and Dýrafjörður fjords, it ensures year-round travel between the northern and southern parts of the region.

MENNO SCHAEFER/SHUTTERSTOCK ©

🗺 How to

Getting here The beginning of the route is 111km from Reykjavík where you turn off the Ring Rd onto Vestfjarðavegur (Rd 60) towards Búðardalur and the Westfjords. To begin from the east and travel anticlockwise, continue on the Ring Rd, turning onto Rd 68 just past the N1 petrol station at Staðarskáli.

When to go The route is open all year, but in winter some roads are not cleared every day. The weather is unpredictable even in the summer, so follow forecasts and road conditions (safetravel.is, road.is, vedur.is).

MAYALL/ULLSTEIN BILD VIA GETTY IMAGES ©

Map locations: Minnibakki, Bolungarvík, Bolafjall, Ísafjörður, Dalbær, Saebol, Naustahvilft, Ögur, Melgraseyri, Suðavík, Svalvogar, Haukadalur, Reykjanes, Kaldbakur, Þingeyri, Heydalur, Hrafnseyri, Bildudalur, Tálknafjörður, Reykjarfjörður, Hvallátur, Flókalundur, Bjarkalundur, Brekkuvellir, Hellulaug, Reykhólar

Left Switchback road on Bolafjall.
Below Bathers in Hellulaug

Sensational Scenery

The landscapes here are so awe-inspiring that drivers need to take care not to get distracted. Be sure to allow enough time for your journey as you're going to make a lot of stops (remember to always park safely). Pack a lunch and stop for a picnic. Among the many highlights is the view from **Bolafjall** in Bolungarvík. Drive to the top of the mountain for panoramic views of Ísafjarðardjúp and Jökulfirðir. At the time of writing, construction of a viewing platform was underway, and the building of services and facilities as well as plans to ensure access beyond the summer months were planned.

Hikers' Heaven

The region is a dream for nature enthusiasts, and you can easily add a few short hikes to your road trip. At 998m, **Kaldbakur** in the so-called Westfjords Alps is the tallest mountain in the region. The hike to its summit – which rewards you with views over Arnarfjörður and Dýrafjörður – takes around four hours, but you'll need a 4WD to reach the trailhead.

While most views are of uninterrupted landscape in this sparsely populated region, those over the town of Ísafjörður and beyond are worth the steep climb. It takes roughly 30 minutes to climb to giant crater-like **Naustahvilft** (the Troll Seat) from just northeast of Ísafjörður airport. For more information, check out vestfjardaleidin.is and @VisitWestfjords.

≋ Soaking It Up

What I love about the Westfjords is the emptiness and ruggedness – and there are so few people. It's like going back in time. There are also quite a few geothermal springs and pools. My favourite is Hellulaug. Taking a dip there is a good start or end to the long drive through the region. The water is also the perfect temperature. Another favourite is the pool and hot spring in Reykjarfjörður near Bíldadalur. In the winter you can sit there in the hot water surrounded by snow and darkness.

By Páll Stefánsson

Páll has been photographing Iceland for 40 years. He has published more than 35 books, is the recipient of numerous awards, and is a Sony Global Imaging Ambassador. He visits the Westfjords four to six times a year. @pallistef

FJORDS
& Landscapes

01 Krossneslaug

Shoreside geothermal pool at the end of the road on Strandir. Uninterrupted views of the North Atlantic.

02 Valagil

Ravine with towering waterfall near Súðavík.

03 Önundarfjörður

Stunning fjord with steep cliffs and a golden-sand beach. The village of Flateyri is located here.

04 Dýrafjörður

Another truly breathtaking fjord. The village of Þingeyri is located here.

05 Drangsnes hot-pots

Hot tubs down at the shoreline in the town of Drangsnes with views into the fjord in front.

06 Rauðasandur (also spelt Rauðisandur)

Long golden-red beach home to birdlife and seals.

07 Svalvogavegur

Narrow, rough coastal road along the mountainside between Dýrafjörður and Arnarfjörður. Only accessible in summer by foot, mountain bike or well-equipped 4WD.

08 Vigur
Island in Ísafjarðardjúp with abundant seabirds. Reached by boat or kayak trip.

09 Reykjafjarðarlaug
Swimming pool and natural hot spring in Reykjafjörður, with views of Arnarfjörður.

10 Dynjandi
Cascading 100m-high waterfall.

11 Látrabjarg
Nesting puffins and other seabirds can be observed up close at the bird cliffs of Látrabjarg.

12 Grímsey
Another island rich in birdlife. Off Drangnes in Steingrímsfjörður. Scheduled boat trips available.

13 Hornbjarg
Dramatic sea cliff and another popular bird-nesting area in remote Hornstrandir. Reached only by boat or multi-day hike.

34 Hornstrandir HIKES

REMOTE | TOURS | LANDSCAPES

Remote Hornstrandir has no roads, shops or permanent inhabitants, and can only be reached by boat or on foot. It also has limited phone connection and few marked hiking trails. But what it does have is remarkable hiking, tall bird cliffs, wildflowers and Arctic foxes. Our itinerary includes a 23km two-day guided hike from Hornvík to Veiðileysufjörður.

AGATHA KADAR/ SHUTTERSTOCK ©

🗺 Trip Notes

Getting here The tour, guided by borea.is, leaves by boat from Ísafjörður.

When to go Early June to mid-September depending on weather.

Tour and ferry operators Borea.is. Other tours/ferries: westtours.is and hornstrandaferdir.is from Bolungarvík, and strandferdir.is from Norðurfjörður.

Safety Experienced hikers embarking on unguided hiking should register a travel plan, bring a GPS, compass and map, and consider a PLB. (safetravel.is)

🐾 Respecting Nature

Hornstrandir is a protected area so stick to the hiking trails. The flora is delicate, and the wildlife needs to be left alone. Drones require a permit from the Environment Agency. Everything you bring into the area you must take out – you can't leave anything behind. Pitch your tent only at designated camping spots.

Ragúel Hagalínsson
Ranger and guide on Hornstrandir.

02 A spectacular bay, **Hornvík** is your arrival point.

03 **Hornbjarg** is one of the North Atlantic's largest bird cliffs.

Fljótavík

Hlöðuvík

Hornvík

Látrar

Aðalvík

Hafnarós

Veiðileysufjörður

Bolungarvík ○

°Hesteyri

04 A steep secluded fjord, **Veiðileysufjörður** offers dramatic vistas across Jökulfirðir on the hike down towards the returning ferry.

Jökulfirðir

Furufjörður ○

Grunnavík

01 Guided tours for the recommended route and ferries depart from **Ísafjörður**. Get any additional gear and food for your trip. Visit the information centre for advice and rent a PLB if planning an unguided trip.

Ísafjarðardjúp

○ Hnífsdalur

Ísafjörður

Ulsfa

N

0 — 10 km
0 — 5 miles

Listings

BEST OF THE REST

 ## Outdoor Adventures

Backcountry Skiing in Hornstrandir

Traverse remote fjords for top skiing with panoramic views in Hornstrandir nature reserve, only reached by boat. Borea Adventures and Aurora Arktika run multi-day ski-to-sailboat tours from Ísafjörður with accommodation on their yachts. Borea also runs tours from its ski lodge on Hornstrandir. If you've got the cash to splash, you won't want to miss this.

Skiing near Ísafjörður

Backcountry skiing tours with Borea are also available in the mountains around Ísafjörður. The Two Valleys (Dalirnir Tvei) ski resort, located 6km from Ísafjörður, is a more affordable option. Tungudalur has three lifts and Seljalandsdalur recommended is for cross-country skiing.

Hiking in Hornstrandir

An alternative to reaching Hornstrandir via Ísafjörður (p210) is to hike or take a boat from Norðurfjörður. Travel along the gravel road in the Westfjords eastern region – it's a two-hour drive from Hólmavík. At the end of the road you will find Norðurfjörður and Krossneslaug pool. From June to August, experienced and well-prepared hikers can hike to Drangaskörð or the pool in Reykjarfjörður and onwards. Boat tours are also available. (strandferdir.is, reykjarfjordur.is, safetravel.is)

 ## Cultural & Artistic Discoveries

Seafood Trail Suðureyri

Guided walking tour with tasting. (fishermaniceland.com)

Jón Sigurðsson Museum

At Hrafnseyri in Arnarfjörður is a museum dedicated to the leader of Iceland's 19th-century independence movement Jón Sigurðsson (1811–79). Enjoy coffee and waffles in the turf house, a replica of the home in which Jón grew up in on the farm. There's a special program on 17 June, Iceland's National Day.

Museum of Sorcery & Witchcraft

This museum in Hólmavík details the history of witch hunts in 17th-century Iceland.

Sheep Farming Museum

Find out about traditional sheep farming in Iceland. Feed the lambs and check out the handicraft store. Located 11km south of Hólmavík.

The Factory Art Exhibition

Check out the annual summer art exhibition in the old fish factory in Djúpavík. The exhibition showcases local and international multidisciplinary artists. Djúpavík is a 75-minute (69km) drive on gravel road from Hólmavík and a natural stop on the way to Krossneslaug.

The Factory Art Exhibition

Samúel Jónsson Art Museum

This colourful museum in Sélardalur over-looking Arnarfjörður consists mostly of quirky outdoor sculptures of people and animals and a church built by artist Samúel Jónsson (1884–1969). It's a 40-minute (20km) drive on a rough gravel road from Bíldudalur.

Museum of Everyday Life

Located in Ísafjörður this museum shares local voices and looks at everyday life in the Westfjords.

Local Wares

The Old Book Store

In operation since 1914, this place in Flateyri is said to be the oldest original store in Iceland. The interior is in its original state and much of the old store equipment is still in use. As its name suggests, it sells mostly (second-hand Icelandic) books, but it also stocks a range of other items like unique postcards, bookmarks and sweets.

Ívaf Knitwear

Locally handmade woollen items like hats, long johns and sweaters in unusual colours. Available from the studio in Ísafjörður and online.

The Fjord People

This studio and co-working space in Ísafjörður runs an online store with unique items like hand-drawn maps of the Westfjords, water-colours, Ívaf woollen goods and a cookbook from Þingeyri cafe Simbahöllin. (fjordpeople.is/shop)

Norður Salt

Sea-salt flakes produced with renewable geothermal energy in Reykhólar. Flavours include blueberry, smoked birch and oak, and liquorice. The company welcomes visitors, who can stop by and peek through the windows to see how the salt crystals are

Norður salt

formed. Available online and in stores across Iceland.

Saltverk Salt

Geothermally produced sea-salt flakes are also made in Reykjanes. Flavours include seaweed, smoked birch, Arctic thyme, liquorice and lava. The company emphasises sustainability and zero carbon emissions from production. Available online and in stores across Iceland.

Sætt & Salt Chocolatier

Sea salt from Saltverk is used in these tempting chocolates made in Súðavík. (@saettogsalt)

Drópi Cod Liver Oil

Cold-processed cod-liver oil is made in Bolungarvík. Containing vitamins and omega-3, cod-liver oil is a staple of the Icelandic diet in part to counter the lack of vitamin D during the dark winter months. Drópi's clean design products come in original, fennel, ginger and spearmint flavours. The products are available online and in stores across Iceland. (dropi.com)

Scan to find more things to do in the Westfjords online

≋ Swims & Soaks

Laugarnes

The pool on the coastline in Laugarnes offers views over Breiðafjörður bay.

Reykhólar Seabaths

Soak in scenic hot sea baths boosted with nurturing seaweed from Breiðafjörður bay. It also sells dry kelp powder, which can be used as a face mask or in your bath at home.

Pollurinn

Another perfectly located set of hot tubs, these in Tálknafjörður. As with many hot pools in the region, upkeep is funded through the visitor donation box. Respect the area, take all trash with you and leave the boombox at home.

✕ Waffles, Seafood & Other Good Things

Dunhagi   €

This restaurant in Tálknafjörður delivers a true taste of the Westfjords in a beautifully restored historic house, with rough-hewn wood floors, comfy booths and vintage photographs. Icelandic lamb, trout fresh from the fjord, and seaweeds and salads picked from the neighbouring beach by the affable owner, Dagný herself, all feature on the locally infused menu. Open May through August.

Simbahöllin   €€

Housed in a restored 1915 general store in Þingeyri, Simbahöllin serves Belgian waffles with homemade rhubarb jam and cream that are definitely worth stopping by for. Open in summer.

Litlibær   €

On Ísafjarðardjúp you'll find one of the Westfjords' most atmospheric eateries tucked inside a 19th century, turf-roofed hut. The owners, born and raised on this Skötufjörður farmstead, whip up tasty heart-shaped waffles with whipped cream and homemade blueberry and raspberry jam. Open mid-May to mid-September.

Tjöruhúsið   €€

For some of the best seafood around, head to this warm, rustic Ísafjörður eatery. The set-course, serve-yourself dinner includes soup, catches of the day (fresh off the boat from the nearby harbour), and desserts such as chocolate mousse. Dinner starts promptly at 7pm; book in advance. Open June to September.

Fisherman   €€

Housed in the Fisherman Hotel in Suðureyri, the meals at this cafe/bistro feature locally sourced ingredients and (unsuprisingly!) fresh-from-the-water seafood. Open evenings in summer.

Stúkuhúsið   €€

The staff at this cool eatery in Patreksfjörður serve up filling salads, chicken soup, Icelandic lamb and their speciality: succulent fish fresh from the fjord outside the window – the cod with hints of wasabi is superb.

HEMIS/ALAMY STOCK PHOTO ©

Pollurinn

Kaffi Norðurfjörður   €€

Settle at a table overlooking the tiny harbour in Norðurfjörður to enjoy produce sourced from the fjords and hills – the Icelandic lamb with Béarnaise sauce and local cod with capers are renowned. Be sure to pre-order breakfast; it includes American pancakes, Icelandic cinnamon-scented oatmeal, bacon and eggs. Open June to August.

Festivals & Celebrations

Swamp Soccer

Also known as Mud Football, or Mýrarboltinn in Icelandic, this is the highlight of the nation-wide Merchant's Weekend festival in Ísafjörður, held on the last weekend of July or the first weekend of August. Everyone is welcome to join and if you don't have a team, you can contact the organisers who will put you in touch with one. Teams make their own uniform with the best dressed awarded a prize. Expect to leave covered in mud. Also includes live concerts from Iceland's top artists.

Simbahöllin

Aldrei fór ég suður Music Festival

Held annually over Easter, the 'I never went south' music festival in Ísafjörður features Icelandic favourites.

Dýrafjarðardagar Festival

Þingeyri's big party is the Dýrafjarðardagar Festival, held on the last weekend of June or the first weekend of July. It features staged fights and celebrates the area's Viking heritage and the saga of local man Gísli Súrsson.

WEST ICELAND

ADVENTURE | OUTDOORS | DINING

Experience
West
Iceland
online

WEST ICELAND
Trip Builder

Explore bookable experiences in West Iceland online

Even for Iceland, the West has a bounty of natural wonders to explore. Enjoy them on foot with a hike up the glacier-capped volcano Snæfellsjökull, on sea with a kayaking tour at the base of Kirkjufell mountain, or from the soothing hot springs near Húsafell.

Hike to the summit of **Snæfellsjökull** glacier (p220)
🕐 ½–1 day

Dine on fresh seafood and explore colourful **Stykkishólmur** and its surrounds (p225)
🕐 3 hours–1 day

Journey to **Langjökull** glacier ice tunnel (p232)
🕐 2–4 hours

Jump aboard a midnight sun kayaking tour in Grundarfjörður for unique views of **Kirkjufell** (p225)
🕐 3 hours

Take in **Hraunfossar** waterfall streaming out of the lava field above; **Barnafoss** waterfall is adjacent (p231)
🕐 1 hour

Walk **Djúpalónssandur** beach with its black pebbles, lava formations and lifting stones (p222)
🕐 1 hour

Stadharholskirkja
Laugarbakki
Skarð
Laugaro
Reykjaskóli
Laugaro
Staðarfell
Stóra-Vatnshorn
Staðarskáli
Stykkishólmur
Búðardaluro
Skjöldur
Erpsstaðir
Hellissandur
Búlandshöfði
Vatnaleið
●Ólafsvík
Grundarfjörður
Vegamóto
Heggstaðir
Búðir
Arnarstapi
Hafffjörður
Birfröst
Fljótstunga
Haugar
Húsafell
Reykholt
Borgarnes
Álftanes○
Melahverfi○
Akranes ●
Reykjavík ✪
Garður○
Hafnarfjörður ●

N
0 — 20 km
0 — 10 miles

Practicalities

ARRIVING

Keflavík International Airport From here you'll pass through Reykjavík. Transit hub Borgarnes is 76km from Reykjavík.

Car and bus Driving is the easiest way to travel the region. Buses (straeto.is) from Reykjavík exist but are infrequent.

FIND YOUR WAY

Snæfellsnes, Snæfellsjökull National Park and Borgarbyggð West Iceland have visitor centres for information.

MONEY

A trip to the local swimming pool is good value for money. There are some great camping spots in the region.

WHERE TO STAY

Town	Pro/Con
Borgarnes	Good base for day trips; plenty of services, facilities and accommodations.
Húsafell	Gateway to the central highlands. Popular camping and summer-house area – also more luxurious options like Hotel Húsafell.
Snæfellsnes Peninsula	Pick the south for views of Snæfellsjökull glacier; the north for more facilities.

GETTING AROUND

Car Driving is the best option unless you're joining tours.

Bus Services (bus.is) run between several towns but are infrequent.

EATING & DRINKING

Dairy Ice cream and *skyr* at Erpsstaðir farm (p232).

Farm food Free-range meats and fresh produce at Bjarteyjarsandur farm (p232) in Hvalfjörður.

Beer Microbrewery Steðji (stedji.com) has tastings.

Slow food Crisscross (crisscross.is) runs tours.

Best located restaurant Hotel Flatey (p225)

Must-try seafood Sjávarpakkhúsið (p233) and Bjargarsteinn Mathús (p233)

JAN–MAR
Possible snowy landscapes and Northern Lights.

APR–MAY
Cooler than summer but less crowded.

JUN–AUG
Long bright days best for hiking.

SEP–DEC
Changing foliage. Northern Lights start. Some places close.

WEST ICELAND FIND YOUR FEET

Journey Up the
GLACIER

NATURAL WONDER | ADVENTURE | VIEWS

On a clear day, the glacier-capped Snæfellsjökull volcano, with its distinct flat-top cone-shaped peak, dominates the skyline for much of the drive from Reykjavík to Snæfellsnes. Hike to its 1446m summit for views stretching from Reykjavík and Reykjanes Peninsula to the south and to the Westfjords to the north. Private ski touring is also an exciting option.

LEOSPEK/SHUTTERSTOCK ©

🗺 How to

Getting here Snæfellsjökull is a 2½-hour drive from Reykjavík.

Expect to pay Snow-cat tours (from 9000kr to 23,000kr); hiking tours (from 15,000kr to 25,000kr); group booking for four to six people for a private ski tour (starting from 45,000kr per person).

Tour operators Hiking (gowest.is), hiking tours from Reykjavík (mountainguides.is), private ski and hiking tours from Reykjavík (asgardbeyond. com), snow cat (sfn.is).

NINA B/SHUTTERSTOCK ©

HARALD NACHTMANN/GETTY IMAGES ©

Clockwise from bottom left Volcanic rocks dot the landscape at Snæfellsjökull; Snæfellsjökull summit hike; Svöðufoss and Snæfellsjökull

Choose Your Own Adventure

The challenging full-day hike up steep and snowy terrain to the glacier's summit – taking six to 12 hours depending on conditions and time of year – will leave you feeling on top of the world. Apart from being the best way to experience the glacier up close, you'll learn all about it from your guide. There are also half-day tours taking you part of the way up. Snow-cat tours (April to August) are also available. From April to June, experienced skiers with their own equipment can ski back down when conditions allow. For groups travelling on a bigger budget, consider private ski touring. Try to visit on a clear day for the vast oceanic views. Glacier crevasses are most impressive in autumn after the summer melt.

Safety First

Joining a tour with an accredited local operator is a must. Your certified guide will fit you with the safety equipment – such as crampons, safety lines and harnesses – necessary for the time of year.

Inspiring Force

Jules Verne's 1864 classic novel *Journey to the Centre of the Earth* and Nobel Prize–winning Icelandic author Halldór Laxness' *Under the Glacier* are among the celebrated works set at the glacier. It is also believed by many to be one of the earth's energy centres.

🌿 Protecting the Environment

Our glacier is melting fast and glaciologists say it will have disappeared by 2050. This glacier is a defining feature of the area, helping to regulate the peninsula's weather, hydrology and biodiversity. It also brings a mystic energy, impacting the wellbeing of locals and visitors alike. If you don't know what I'm talking about, give it a chance! When it comes to the environment, everything we do has an impact. You can, for example, use your own energy to climb the glacier and offset your trip through tree planting via the Iceland Carbon Fund.

Jón Jóel Einarsson
Jón first climbed Snæfellsjökull in 1975 and started guiding a few years later. He is passionate about environmental sustainability and a strong believer in the positive impacts of eco-tourism. He is co-founder and co-owner of Go West. @gowesticeland

Snæfellsnes Natural
WONDERS

01 Djúpalónssandur

Cove of pearl-like smooth black pebbles lined with lava formations that lies within Snæfellsnes National Park.

02 Gatklettur

Natural rock arch on birdlife abundant coastline near Arnarstapi.

03 Breiðafjörður

Bay with innumerable islands and skerries separating Snæfellsnes and the Westfjords. Home to rich bird and marine life.

04 Kirkjufell and Kirkjufellsfoss

Kirkjufell mountain (463m) famously appeared in the TV series *Game of Thrones*. Kirkjufellsfoss waterfall is located near its base.

05 Löngufjörur

Among the country's few golden – rather than black – sand beaches, Löngufjörur has a Snæfellsjökull backdrop and is popular among horse riders.

06 Gerðuberg

Hillside row of 15m basalt columns.

07 Svörtuloft

Lighthouse atop breathtaking cliffs.

08 Berserkjahraun

Moss-covered lava field with colourful craters.

09 Ytri-Tunga

Prime spot for observing seals.

10 Snæfellsjökull

Glacier-topped 1446m stratovolcano and the region's crown jewel. Glacier has been rapidly retreating and could be gone by mid-century.

11 Búðavík bay

Best viewed from down by the shore near the black wooden church or from Hotel Búðir where you may spy seals in the estuary.

12 Svöðufoss

Snæfellsjökull looms above this waterfall.

13 Lóndrangar

Towering basalt sea stacks of up to 75m resembling castles. Summer nesting site for puffins.

36 Adventures
AT SEA

KAYAKING | WILDLIFE | RELAXATION

■■■■ Visitors to West Iceland and Snæfellsnes are spoilt for choice, so it's easy to overlook the adventures that await at sea. Spectacular Breiðafjörður bay is home to rich bird and marine life, not to mention history and landscapes. Separating Snæfellsnes and the Westfjords, its countless islands are today mostly abandoned. Join a kayak or sailing tour, or take the ferry to Flatey island.

ARCTIC IMAGES/GETTY IMAGES ©

🗺 How to

Getting here Boat tours leave from Ólafsvík, Grundarfjörður and Stykkishólmur on the northern side of Snæfellsnes.

When to go From May to September most tours operate and Flatey hotel and restaurant are open. Some companies offer year-round tours.

Tour operators The following offer a variety of kayaking, boating, fishing and wildlife-watching tours: kontiki.is, lakitours. is, oceanadventures.is, seatours.is, vesturadventures.is.

What to wear Warm clothes and sunglasses.

FEIFEI CUI-PAOLUZZO/GETTY IMAGES ©

Flatey

Brjánslækur
Bjarkalundur

Reykhólar

Stadharholskirkja

Skarð

Staðarfell

Breiðafjörður

Stykkishólmur

Skjöldur

Hellissandur
Kirkjufell
Vatnaleið

Ólafsvik
Grundarfjörður

0 — 20 km
0 — 10 miles

Top Whale watchers spot an orca, Breiðafjörður bay **Bottom** Cod drying, Flatey

Kayaking at Kirkjufell The most popular viewpoint for the iconic Kirkjufell mountain is by the waterfall near its base. To experience the mountain from another perspective, join a kayaking tour out into Grundarfjörður fjord. You'll paddle along the coastline where you'll see the mountain from different angles. Keep an eye out for seals. In summer, take the evening tour in the magic of the midnight sun. Tours are two to three hours. Kayak fishing and customised private tours, which can include a beach BBQ, are also available.

Setting out from Stykkishólmur Kayaking tours also run along the coastline near Stykkishólmur. You'll search for puffins, eagles and seals, see an abandoned shipwreck or paddle out towards Breiðafjörður's islands.

Watching for whales and puffins Other on-water options include the Viking Sushi nature and birdwatching tour from Stykkishólmur with fresh shellfish tasting. There are also sea angling, nature and whale-watching tours in the area.

Island retreat Flatey – not to be confused with the island of the same name in North Iceland – is the only year-round inhabited island on Breiðafjörður bay. In the summer, the old colourful timber houses, mostly built in the early 1900s, serve as summer cabins. The island is just 2km by 500m. No cars, no shops – just you and nature. The restaurant attracts visitors for its fresh local ingredients, like fish, mussels, lumpfish caviar and seaweed. The ferry takes 1½ hours from Stykkishólmur and continues on to Brjánslækur in the Westfjords.

Escape to Flatey

Flatey is all about getting away from the hustle and bustle of the modern world. I live in LA, but I come here for three or four months a year to just check out. There isn't a lot to do here and that's the point. Time becomes irrelevant. You can take walks around the island. It's known for its birdlife, so we get a lot of birdwatchers. Check out the murals at the church. And then you can, of course, come to the hotel and have one of the best meals you'll have in Iceland!

Friðgeir Trausti Helgason
Friðgeir is an Icelandic chef and photographer. He lives in the US but spends most of his summers working as head chef at Hotel Flatey.
@kokkageiri

37 On the Saga
TRAIL

HISTORY | SAGAS | PIONEERS

West Iceland is where some of the most famous explorers and saga heroes lived. This is where their stories were told, retold and written down. This is where saga author Snorri Sturluson lived, worked and met his bitter end. When touring the Sagaland, pay close attention: their stories are inscribed into stones and echo among the mountains.

IMAGEBROKER/OLAF KRUEGER/GETTY IMAGES ©

🔖 How to

Getting around It's best to hire a car at Keflavík International Airport or in Reykjavík. Infrequent public buses (straeto.is) run from Reykjavík to the region.

When to go Year-round, but some museums are only open in summer.

Top tip Download the Locatify SmartGuide app from App Store or Play Store. The GPS navigation system will detect your location and provide you with insights into your surroundings – like a personal guide. You can also listen to it before you arrive.

NICK FOX/SHUTTERSTOCK ©

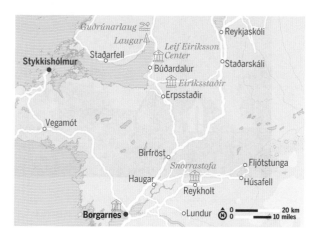

Top Replica of a Viking long-house, Eiríksstaðir **Bottom** Guðrúnarlaug hot spring

Living history Get cosy by the long-fire in Eiríksstaðir, a longhouse replica in Haukadalur, and listen to storytellers clad in Viking clothing tell tales of the people who lived there. This is where Eiríkur Rauði and his wife Þjóðhildur built their farm and founded their family. They later became the first Nordic people to settle in Greenland.

Viking voyages Dedicated to explorers Eiríkur and his son Leifur Heppni ('the Lucky'), the Leif Eiriksson Center in Búðardalur traces the story of *Grænlendinga saga*, documenting their exploration of Greenland and North America. According to the saga, Leifur arrived in America in the year 1000 – 500 years before Columbus. Written sources are backed by archaeological evidence.

Lethal love triangle Visit Laugar in Sælingsdalur, the lush countryside where the *Laxdæla Saga* took place. Bathe in Guðrúnarlaug, built to resemble the pool where heroine Guðrún Ósvífursdóttir soaked with her suitors, neither of whom foresaw the bloody end to their love story.

Skaldic warrior The Settlement Centre in Borgarnes is dedicated to Egill Skallagrímsson, a poet, warrior and one of the most colourful characters of the Icelandic sagas. The exhibition recounts the magical and mythical storyline of *Egil's Saga*. Another exhibition explains how the Norse explorers navigated across open ocean, why they abandoned their homes and what awaited them in this new, uninhabited country. In the centre's loft, storytelling events and monologues are held. The restaurant offers scrumptious buffets.

🏠 Snorri's Home

In Snorrastofa (p228), about 90 minutes north of Reykjavík, learn about the career and political influence of Snorri Sturluson, one of the most famous Icelanders who ever lived. Not only did Snorri have a strong impact on the political and cultural life in Iceland while he was alive, but his literary masterpieces – *Snorra-Edda*, *Heimskringla* and (most likely) *Egils saga* – have continued to shape the culture and self-image of Icelanders and Nordic people to this day. Snorri's pool has been maintained, along with part of the tunnel which connected it to his house, which are some of the oldest preserved structures in Iceland.

Sagaland

WHERE HISTORY WAS MADE

During the commonwealth, West Iceland was the richest and most populated region in Iceland. Most of the Icelandic sagas were written in the region, including *Egil's Saga*, *Sturlunga Saga*, *Laxdæla Saga* and *Eyrarbyggja Saga*, and many of the most powerful chieftains and notable characters lived here.

Left Church in Reykholt **Middle** 14th century manuscript of Snorri Sturluson's *Prose Edda* **Right** Sculptor Gustav Vigeland's statue of Snorri Sturluson

'It's the cradle of the country's literary tradition. There are many theories as to why that was. Writing manuscripts was expensive and this was the wealthiest region, maybe because of trade with Greenland, among other reasons', says Sigrún Þormar, service director at Snorrastofa. This cultural and medieval centre is based in Reykholt where Snorri Sturluson lived and worked in the 13th century.

Poetry, Fantasy & Adventure

'He wrote *Snorra-Edda*, poetry about Norse mythology, which has had a great influence on Western culture. It's everywhere. For example, the television series *Vikings* and *Game of Thrones*, the *Lord of the Rings* trilogy and Marvel cartoons are all under the influence of Norse mythology.' Snorri was a Christian, but he was interested in pre-Christian religion, myths, worldview and poetry. '*Snorra-Edda* is really about fantasy and adventure', says Sigrún. Snorri based his writing on older manuscripts, ancient poetry and oral stories about the gods, and his own imagination. 'Nobody had written anything like this before.'

Snorri also chronicled the history of the Norwegian kings in the so-called *Heimskringla* and most likely wrote *Egil's Saga*, the first major Icelandic saga. 'It was probably the last book that he wrote. It was the biography of Egill Skallagrímsson who lived at Borg in Borgarnes, and he was one of the very few real Icelandic Vikings. Egill went to Norway and England for raids, and was in the service of the English king as a soldier. But he always returned to Iceland to his farm. He was also a loving father and husband – and extremely ugly!' laughs Sigrún.

Pioneer & Businessman

Snorri had his own pool to bathe in, channelling water 120m from a nearby hot spring. 'Maybe he sat in his hot-pot in Reykholt, looked at the stars, Northern Lights and Milky Way and fantasised about the gods above', suggests Sigrún. The original pool has been maintained and part of the tunnel that connected it to the house. Snorri also heated one room with the steam from the hot spring, possibly for brewing or to use as a sauna. Around the house was a fort, for defence, and perhaps also to show off his wealth. 'The money came from the women he married. He knew how to pick them! But he was also a clever businessman.' Snorri received additional financial support from his family. He financed his own book production so could write what he wanted.

> History is all around... It's fascinating. It makes the story so real – because it's not just a story.

In Snorrastofa, visitors can learn about the life and work of Snorri Sturluson. History is all around, says Sigrún. 'I once went riding along Hvítá river, past the remains of a turf house that dates back to the 9th or 10th century.' Sources and archaeological evidence indicate that this was where Skallagrímur, Egill's father, first settled after arriving from Norway. 'It's so adventurous to ride past those remains and consider that this was where Skallagrímur came with all his belongings, wife, children, slaves and farmhands after the king had killed his son. It's fascinating. It makes the story so real – because it's not just a story.'

📖 Inspirational Characters

Auður djúpúðga (the 'deep-minded') was the only woman to lead a settlement expedition to Iceland. Escaping the escalating conflict in Britain, she settled in Hvammur in Dalir. Auður was a Christian and freed all her slaves.

Guðríður víðförla (the 'far-travelled') was among the first Icelandic settlers in Greenland and she later went on an expedition to North America where her son Snorri was born. Late in life, she went on a pilgrimage to Rome.

Geirmundur heljarskinn (the 'black-skinned') was described as 'the most noble of all settlers', yet his story is largely unknown. Author and scholar Bergsveinn Birgisson reasons that he was of Siberian descent and that he built an empire around walrus hunting.

38 Hiking in the **WEST**

MOUNTAINS | FORESTS | WATERFALLS

West Iceland has an abundance of hiking opportunities, from lava fields and mountain vistas to green hills and forests, and glacial landscapes and waterfalls.

🗺 How to

Getting around Hire a car at Keflavík International Airport or in Reykjavík, or join a tour. Infrequent public buses (straeto.is) run from Reykjavík to the region.

When to go Summer and autumn are the best and safest seasons for hiking.

What to bring Warm and waterproof clothing, and good hiking boots. Lip balm and sunscreen, plus water and food for longer walks.

Top tip Wapp (wapp.is) is a free app with GPS tracks for hiking, detailed maps and other info.

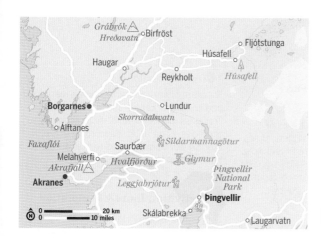

Top Grábrók's ancient volcanic crater
Bottom Hraunfossar

Ancient Routes

Síldarmannagötur This means 'herring people street' and connects Hvalfjörður and Skorradalur. The name comes from the time when herring was caught in Hvalfjörður. The route begins at a parking space in the innermost part of the fjord.
Distance 14km | Elevation 450m | Time 5hr | Level Medium

Leggjabrjótur The name translates to 'leg breaker' but refers to horses rather than people. It leads from Hvalfjörður to the parliament in Þingvellir. Start at Þingvellir for a breathtaking view on the way down to Hvalfjörður.
Distance 16km | Elevation 500m | Time 6hr | Level Medium

Note that both routes lead from one area to another, so hikers need someone to drop them off and pick them up. Bus services (re.is) are sometimes available for these routes.

Hills & Mountains

Grábrók (170m) An ancient volcanic crater right on the Ring Rd by Bifröst. It's an easy walk for the entire family. Look down into the crater and admire the view of the surrounding lava field, Hreðavatn lake and cone-shaped mountain Baula.
Distance 1km | Elevation 70m | Time 30min | Level Easy

Akrafjall (643m) Head towards Akranes on Rd 51, but instead of driving into town, take a right and another right towards the mountain. From the top, there's a magnificent panoramic view, including of Faxaflói bay and Reykjavík.
Distance 5km | Elevation 500m | Time 3hr | Level Medium

Waterfalls & Wondrous Nature

At 198m **Glymur waterfall** in Hvalfjörður is the country's second-highest. A sign indicates the parking area. The trail is marked. For a better view of the waterfall, cross Botnsá river before moving up. The path is steep, but the view is worth it.
Distance 7km | Elevation 300m | Time 3hr | Level Medium

At the edge of Langjökull glacier, in the innermost part of Borgarfjörður, lies the forested area of **Húsafell**, with a hotel, campground and cottages. Find myriad marked hiking trails, of various lengths and levels, to natural attractions, including **Hraunfossar** and **Barnafoss** waterfalls.

Listings

BEST OF THE REST

Farm Visits & Family Fun

Hólar Petting Farm

Kids and adults alike delight in the close encounters with horses, dogs, rabbits, sheep and goats. The farm also has a cow and a pig, as well as some birds. The locals show guests around the farm and introduce them to farm work. Open mid-June to mid-August.

Erpsstaðir Dairy Farm

Your one-stop shop for dreamy dairy. Visit the Erpsstaðir creamery and try homemade ice cream, cheeses, *skyr* (yoghurt-like dessert) and *skyr* pralines. Observe the cows being milked and learn about milk production.

Bjarteyjarsandur Family Farm

Visit an authentic sheep farm and its 600 sheep and other animals. Learn all about farm work and how it varies from season to season. In addition to free-range lamb, the farm produces free-range pork, poultry and organic vegetables.

The Icelandic Goat Centre

Háafell is one of the largest goat farms in Iceland. The Icelandic Goat Centre, which is based at Háafell, was established to protect and maintain the Icelandic Settlement Goat – a special breed. Visit and pet the friendly goats; learn more about their qualities and goat-related products.

Sturlureykir Horse Farm

A horse-breeding farm with 60 horses, Sturlureykir offers horseback-riding tours and stable visits. Meet the horses and learn more about the special Icelandic breed, including its five gaits. The farm has a hot spring where rye bread is baked.

Troll Park at Fossatún

Fossatún offers accommodation, a restaurant and an activity centre, and is located by the Tröllafoss falls. All around are trolls who have turned to stone, at least according to proprietor Steinar Berg, who has written several books about them. Walk along the 'troll trail' and play 'troll games' in the park.

Activities, Tours & Exploration

Löngufjörur Beach Ride

Riding a good Icelandic horse on the smooth white sands of Löngufjörur – especially in the special gaits *tölt* and flying pace – is a divine experience. Feel the sun on your face and the wind in your hair, while listening to the waves and watching the pristine white ice cap of Snæfellsjökull in the distance. Find tour operators online. (west.is)

Langjökull Tours

Iceland's second-largest glacier is a world full of wonder waiting to be explored, inside and out! Join a snowmobile or super-Jeep tour and whoosh across the frozen surface. Afterwards enter the world's largest artificial ice tunnel.

Langjökull glacier tunnel

Cave Explorations

Join tours to visit **Vatnshellir** and **Víðgelmir**, ancient lava tubes, and discover the ice sculptures and stone formations of 'the underworld'. **Surtshellir** is another famous cave near Víðgelmir, which used to be a hideout for outlaws. Wear good shoes, helmet and headlight and don't disturb your surroundings.

Angling

In West Iceland there's an abundance of rivers and lakes for fishing salmon, trout and sea trout. The price varies greatly, and it can be difficult to get access to the most expensive salmon rivers. However, fishing in lakes is more affordable. (veidikortid.is)

 ## Swimming & Soaking

Borgarnes Geothermal Pool

Right on the Ring Rd, the geothermal pool in Borgarnes has great facilities for people who like to exercise, relax and play. It has a wading pool for kids and waterslides.

Akranes & Guðlaug Geothermal Pools

Jaðarsbakkalaug is a family-friendly 25m outdoor pool in Akranes with hot tubs, a steam bath and waterslide. On Langisandur beach is the cleverly designed three-level Guðlaug Natural Pool, loved by sea swimmers and wonderful for relaxing. Entrance is free.

Lýsuhólslaug Geothermal Bath

This old country pool is filled with naturally hot mineral water rich in green algae and various minerals that are considered to have healing properties. From the pool, bathers can enjoy the view of Lýsuhyrna mountain.

Húsafell Pool & Canyon Baths

In Húsafell is a geothermal pool with hot tubs and a waterslide. You can also join a two-hour guided hiking and bathing tour to the Húsafell Canyon Baths. The trail leads past natural wonders, including Langifoss waterfall.

Vatnshellir cave

Krauma Geothermal Baths & Spa

A mix of water from Deildartunguhver, Europe's most powerful hot spring, and glacial water is the recipe for a relaxing soak in Krauma. Additionally, it has a cold tub, two saunas and a relaxation room where guests can doze off by the fireplace.

 ## A Taste of West Iceland

Sjávarpakkhúsið   €€

Working with fishers, farmers and brewers to source the best local materials, this small seafood restaurant is located at Stykkishólmur harbour. The mussels (when in season) and scallops from Breiðafjörður bay are highlights. Get a window seat for the views.

Bjargarsteinn Mathús   €€

Another gem serving locally sourced and seasonal ingredients. Located in a small beautifully renovated house from 1908 at the waterfront in Grundarfjörður, this restaurant boasts views of Kirkjufell. The fish of the day, seaweed innovations and desserts are standouts.

 Scan to find more things to do in West Iceland online

Practicalities

ARRIVING

236

GETTING AROUND

238

SAFE TRAVEL

240

MONEY

241

RESPONSIBLE TRAVEL

242

ACCOMMODATION

244

ESSENTIALS

246

LANGUAGE

248

Right Winter hikers walking on ice glacier

EASY STEPS FROM THE AIRPORT TO THE CITY CENTRE

Most travellers who come to Iceland enter through Keflavík International Airport. It's approximately 50km from Reykjavík or a 45-minute drive. The airport is rather small and compact, with only one passenger terminal, but is being expanded. There are a variety of shops, restaurants and services, including ATMs and car-hire desks. Domestic flights go from Reykjavík Domestic Airport.

AT THE AIRPORT

SIM Cards
Tourists can purchase cards in the 24-hour convenience store in the arrival hall and at the Elko electronics store before baggage claim. The largest telecom companies are Síminn, Vodafone and Nova, and SIM cards are also available in their stores.

International Currency Exchange
Available at Arion Bank, which provides currency exchange at its service points in the arrival and departure hall. Note that the exchange rate is less favourable at the airport than at the bank's other branches.

TONY ARRUZA/GETTY IMAGES ©

WI-FI
Free, unlimited and open at the airport. Just connect to Kefairport-FreeWifi

ATMS
There are 14 ATMs – eight in the departure lounge and six in the arrival hall.

CHARGING STATIONS
Available at numerous points around the airport.

CUSTOMS REGULATIONS
The maximum allowance of alcohol per person is six units (one unit is six large beers, one wine bottle, or 0.25L of spirits) and one carton of cigarettes or 250g of other tobacco. Travellers may import duty-free up to 10kg of food not exceeding the value of 25,000kr, excluding meat and dairy products from outside the European Economic Area (EEA).

GETTING TO THE CITY CENTRE

Flybus and **Airport Direct** offer airport transfers to bus terminals in Reykjavík 24/7. Tickets can be booked online with possible hotel connections. The pick-up point is outside the arrivals hall. Booking tickets in advance is recommended: re.is/tour/flybus, airportdirect.is.

Public buses operated by Strætó (straeto.is) run between Keflavík International Airport and the BSÍ bus terminal in Reykjavík with a stop in Keflavík (Rte 55), but less frequently and not 24/7. Tickets cost less for children and the elderly. The bus station is near the P1 parking area.

HOW MUCH FOR A

Taxi
16,500kr
45min

Airport transfer
3290kr
45min

Public bus
1960kr
75min

Taxi
They congregate outside the arrivals hall and can be booked online (including on taxi.booking.com). There are also apps.

Plan Your Journey
Useful apps include Vedur (for weather), Strætó (for public buses), 112 Iceland (for emergencies) and Iceland Road Guide.

Rental Cars
Four car-rental companies have service desks in the Keflavík International Airport arrivals hall. Reykjavík Domestic Airport, 45 minutes from Keflavík, is the hub for domestic travel. Flybus offers tickets to the main terminal in Reykjavík, from which Icelandair flies. Eagle Air flies from a different location. Find travel advice at visiticeland.com/plan-your-trip.

OTHER POINTS OF ENTRY

Smyril Line Ferry MS *Norröna* sails from Hirtshals in Denmark to Seyðisfjörður in Iceland via Tórshavn in the Faroe Islands year-round. The journey takes four days. For a family of four with one vehicle, a round-trip costs approximately 280,000kr.

Flights to/from Greenland Icelandair operates scheduled flights to destinations in west and south Greenland from Reykjavík Airport, and Norlandair flies to east Greenland from Akureyri Airport.

TRANSPORT TIPS TO HELP YOU GET AROUND

The best way to explore Iceland is by car. Car rentals and fuel are expensive, but they allow you to travel at your own pace, make detours and visit remoter regions. You can also take a public bus between the major hubs of each region and fly domestically. Or join a tour and let someone else do the planning.

CAR HIRE

Car hire is available in larger towns. The largest selection of rental-car companies is at Keflavík International Airport. Make sure your contract includes unlimited kilometres. Outside summer, it's best to hire a 4WD. If driving in the highlands, make sure the car is equipped for it.

AUTOMOBILE ASSOCIATIONS

The Icelandic Automobile Association, FÍB (fib. is), is a non-profit organisation and a member of FIA, the worldwide organisation of automobile associations. Members are entitled to various benefits, such as emergency services, legal advice, technical and travelling assistance.

CAR RENTAL PER DAY

from 15,000kr

Petrol approx 250kr/litre

Charging station 40kr/min

ROAD CONDITIONS

Iceland's Ring Rd and most main roads are paved. On gravel roads it's necessary to slow down; some don't have winter service. F-roads are for larger 4WD vehicles in summer only (safetravel.is, vegagerdin.is).

INSURANCE

Make sure you have insurance that covers damages to vehicles and personal injury from your insurance company or credit-card company at home. Car rentals offer additional insurances, including gravel protection.

DRIVING ESSENTIALS

90 — Outside urban areas the speed limit is 90km/h on paved roads; 80km/h on gravel.

EINBREID BRÚ — The first car to arrive at single-lane bridges has right of way.

MALBIK ENDAR — Slow down when crossing from paved roads to gravel or the tires might lose grip.

Look out for sheep, birds and reindeer on the road.

STOP — The maximum legal blood-alcohol level for drivers is 0.02%.

A campervan is an ideal mode of transport for travelling around Iceland in the summer. Campgrounds are ubiquitous all around the country, in practically every town and village, as well as in forests, national parks and around natural and historical sites. Most campgrounds have excellent services and often playgrounds. Visit tjalda.is for an overview of campgrounds.

FERRY

There are scheduled ferry services (road.is/travel-info/ferries) from Landeyjahöfn to Heimaey island (Vestmannaeyjar), from Reykjavík to Viðey island, from Stykkishólmur to Brjánslækur in the Westfjords via Flatey island, from Dalvík to Grímsey island, from Árskógssandur to Hrísey island and from Neskaupstaður to Mjóifjörður (in winter).

PLANE

Icelandair flies from Reykjavík Domestic Airport to Akureyri (where there are connections with Norlandair to other towns), Ísafjörður, Egilsstaðir and Vestmannaeyjar. Eagle Air flies from Reykjavík Domestic (from a different location) to Húsavík and Höfn.

BUS

Strætó (straeto.is) runs between Reykjavík and Akureyri with stops along the way. Services to other areas are infrequent. The main towns have public bus services. SBA offers scheduled buses between Reykjavík and Akureyri.

KNOW YOUR CARBON FOOTPRINT

The Iceland Carbon Fund (ICF) offers carbon offsets through tree planting. Find a carbon calculator (reiknivél) online (kolvidur.is). You can also calculate the carbon footprint of your flight at Icelandair (icelandair.com/carbon-calculator). One adult who travels three hours both ways by air must plant five trees.

ROAD DISTANCE CHART (KM)

	Reykjavík	Egilsstaðir	Ísafjörður	Blönduós	Selfoss	Húsavík	Stykkishólmur	Höfn	Vík	Akureyri
Reykjavík	–									
Egilsstaðir	636	–								
Ísafjörður	455	804	–							
Blönduós	244	391	412	–						
Selfoss	56	577	495	285	–					
Húsavík	463	219	631	219	503	–				
Stykkishólmur	172	600	152	209	213	430	–			
Höfn	456	254	895	576	400	404	613	–		
Vík	184	517	623	413	130	632	342	272	–	
Akureyri	388	248	558	144	428	75	353	502	556	–

ICELAND GETTING AROUND

DANGERS, ANNOYANCES & SAFETY

The weather is the biggest safety hazard for travellers in Iceland. It can be unpredictable, especially in winter. Remember to check the weather forecast and road conditions regularly and take weather warnings seriously.

SNOW & STORMS

Weather warnings are regularly issued because of gale force winds, especially in autumn and winter but they can occur in all seasons. They are particularly hazardous when combined with snowfall. Blizzards block the visibility of drivers and make roads impassable, especially across mountain passes.

AVALANCHES, LANDSLIDES & ROCKFALL

In mountainous areas certain weather conditions create a risk of avalanches, landslides and rockfall, sometimes causing damage or even fatalities. Barriers protect parts of roads and inhabited areas but pay attention to danger alerts and carry avalanche safety gear when mountain skiing.

VOLCANIC & GEOTHERMAL ACTIVITY

Iceland has about 130 active volcanoes. Usually, eruptions occur outside inhabited areas and people are not in danger. Seismic activity is common but major earthquakes are rare. At geothermal areas be careful around hot springs and mud pools. Stay on defined paths or you might suffer serious burns.

COVID-19

The vast majority of the Icelandic population has been vaccinated against Covid-19, but some gathering restrictions remain. For up-to-date information, go to covid.is.

INSURANCE

Persons from the European Economic Area (EEA) must bring their EHIC card to be entitled to healthcare. Persons from outside the EEA must pay for medical assistance in full and can seek reimbursement afterwards.

SAFETY OUTDOORS

When hiking, leave a travel plan (safetravel.is/travel-plan) or rent a PLB (Personal Locator Beacon). Check the forecast. Bring suitable clothing, safety equipment, a map, compass and GPS. In case of emergency, call 112.

The official source for safe adventure in Iceland

SAFETRAVEL.IS

Run by the Icelandic Association for Search and Rescue. Info, weather and road conditions. Sign up for SMS updates and download the safety app 112 Iceland.

QUICK TIPS TO HELP YOU MANAGE YOUR MONEY

CREDIT CARDS
Widely accepted and often preferred over cash. However, occasionally cash is required, for example, at outdoor markets or at natural pools where there's no service and bathers are asked to put money in a box for upkeep. There are ATMs in all towns. Visa and MasterCard are most common, while American Express and Diner's Club are not accepted everywhere.

PAYING THE BILL
It's common to pay for your bill at the counter at cafes, bars and restaurants, even when they have table service.

TIPPING
Completely optional. The total on your bill is all you need to pay and you're not expected to tip your taxi driver or guide.

CURRENCY

Icelandic króna

HOW MUCH FOR A

Cappuccino
650kr

Pint of beer
1300kr

Dinner for two
16,000kr

BANKS & ATMS
At least one of the three largest banks (Arion Bank, Íslandsbanki and Landsbanki) will have a branch and ATMs in larger towns. Smaller towns have none but aren't usually far from larger hubs.

VAT REFUND
Those with permanent residency outside Iceland may be refunded the VAT on purchases made in Iceland. Ask for a form at the counter and claim your VAT refund at Arion Bank at Keflavík Airport.

MONEY CHANGERS
Changing foreign currency is usually no problem at banks (open weekdays, 9am to 4pm). Arion Bank at Keflavík International Airport is open for all morning and afternoon flights.

ON A BUDGET
Granted, Iceland is expensive, and to some people, shockingly so. If you're travelling on a budget, camping is an option, costing 1500kr to 2000kr per adult per night. The price for a dorm bed at a hostel is about 3000kr to 5000kr. Hiking and DIY nature exploration are free. Buy your food at supermarkets and drink tap water. Admission to swimming pools is approximately 1000kr per adult (multi-trip passes are often available) and to heritage museums 2000kr per adult.

DISCOUNTS & SAVINGS
Most sights, activities and public-transport services are offered at reduced rates (or free) to seniors, young children and families. There are some passes and discount cards, including the Reykjavík City Card (visitreykjavik.is), Camping Card (utilegukortid.is), Fishing Card (veidikortid.is) and 5x5 Iceland Ski Pass (available at resorts).

RESPONSIBLE TRAVEL

Tips to leave a lighter footprint, support local and have a positive impact on local communities.

ON THE ROAD

Calculate your carbon at kolvidur.is.

Hire electric or hybrid cars; there are charging stations around the country.

Public buses are generally more ecofriendly than private vehicles and often run on green energy.

Carpool. Check samferda.is.

Cycle. In Reykjavík you can hire a bike, e-bike or e-scooter through apps such as Hopp and Wind.

Verify eco-credentials by looking out for the green Vakinn logo, the Nordic Swan logo and the EU Ecolabel.

Flying drones is forbidden in national parks.

Disinfect. Infectious diseases can be transferred to Icelandic animals, for example, with riding clothing, so disinfect things prior to arrival (mast.is).

GIVE BACK

Volunteer with the Iceland Conservation Volunteers, Thórsmörk Trail Volunteers, Worldwide Friends or SEEDS – if you have time. (Make sure that you're volunteering for a non-profit; see volunteering.is.)

Plogging (called *plokka* in Iceland) is picking up rubbish while exercising.

Head-to-tail cooking is catching on in Iceland. Look out for dishes at restaurants that strive to make use of food that would otherwise have gone to waste.

Make a donation to Landvernd (landvernd.is), Iceland's leading environmental NGO, or the Icelandic Association for Search and Rescue (ICE-SAR; icesar.com), a non-profit, non-commercial, volunteer-based organisation.

DOS & DON'TS

Don't drive off-road, stray from marked trails, walk across sensitive vegetation or camp outside designated areas.

Do close all gates behind you. Otherwise farm animals might escape.

Don't attempt to pet or feed animals, wild or domestic, unless given permission.

LEAVE A SMALL FOOTPRINT

Build your own base camp. Consider picking a specific region to explore. Book a cottage or camp at a campground in your region of choice, and go on hikes and tours from there. Eat and shop locally.

When booking tours, consider the carbon footprint of horseback riding, biking, hiking, skiing and kayaking compared to tours using motorised vehicles.

Green sailing. In Húsavík, North Sailing offers whale watching and other tours on sailboats powered by green energy.

MATEUSZ OZIK/SHUTTERSTOCK ©

SUPPORT LOCAL

Support local businesses in small towns by booking accommodation and tours run by locals and buying products and handicrafts from the area.

Eat locally. Get tips from Slow Food Iceland (slowfood.is/slow-food-guide) on where to find good local food across the country.

CLIMATE CHANGE & TRAVEL

It's impossible to ignore the impact we have when travelling, and the importance of making changes where we can. Lonely Planet urges all travellers to engage with their travel carbon footprint. There are many carbon calculators online that allow travellers to estimate the carbon emissions generated by their journey; try resurgence.org/resources/carbon-calculator.html. Many airlines and booking sites offer travellers the option of offsetting the impact of greenhouse gas emissions by contributing to climate-friendly initiatives around the world. We continue to offset the carbon footprint of all Lonely Planet staff travel, while recognising this is a mitigation more than a solution.

RESOURCES
landvernd.is
visiticeland.com/pledge
vakinn.is

ICELAND POSITIVE-IMPACT TRAVEL

UNIQUE & LOCAL WAYS TO STAY

From a modest tent to caravans, glamping, cottages, farmstay and luxury lodges, Iceland has a range of options for an enjoyable country holiday. In towns and villages, choose between classic hotels and guesthouses, self-service apartments, special-themed stays and boutique accommodation.

HOW MUCH FOR A NIGHT IN

A campsite 4000kr

A cottage 30,000kr

A luxury lodge 60,000kr

GLAMPING

The 'glamorous camping' hype is catching on in Iceland, too. There are igloos, domes and bubbles, luxury tents and Mongolian yurts in various secluded locations in South and North Iceland, adding more comfort and elegance to the camping experience. The price varies, but one night for two persons ranges from 20,000kr to 55,000kr.

NATURE RESERVES & NATIONAL PARKS

Experience nature with all your senses. Crawl into your sleeping bag, listen to the rustling stream and tweeting birds, and smell the wild vegetation. Prepare for bright but cool nights; bring woollen undies and a sleeping mask. Find epic hiking trails in Ásbyrgi, Vesturdalur and Skaftafell; historical sites at Þingvellir National Park; and geothermal wonders at Landmannalaugar. All campgrounds have good facilities. The price is 1500kr to 2000kr per adult per night. Note that biting midges have become a nuisance in South, West and North Iceland.

CAMPERVANS

Campervans don't cost much more than a hire car and allow for complete flexibility. Some are suited for highland roads. They seat and sleep two to five people – and take the hassle out of camping. The average daily price ranges from 20,000kr to 30,000kr. Campervan rentals are available at Keflavík International Airport, among other places.

FARMSTAY

Farmers all around Iceland welcome visitors to their homes. Accommodation is offered in cottages, farmhouses or even renovated stables and barns. The level of service and experience varies. Visitors are invited to observe or take part in farm work, pet the animals, go horseback riding and taste the food produced at the farm. The Wilderness Centre at the edge of the eastern highlands takes its guests on a journey through the past, as they can sleep in a 'museum'. The price varies, but a double room at a farm is usually about 30,000kr per night.

SUMARBÚSTAÐUR

Icelanders love their *sumar-bústa∂ur* (country cottages). There they enjoy the peaceful countryside, sunbathe, pick wild berries and relax with a beer in their hot tub under the stars. Many families own a cottage, but they can also be rented from labour unions. Travellers can rent them, too, and experience a true Icelandic-style holiday. The price varies greatly, but cottages are usually an affordable option for groups. For a twist on the *sumarbústa∂ur* experience, try the huts in Mjóeyri (pictured), 'beer barrels' in Vestmannaeyjar or camping pods in Fossatún.

ICELAND ACCOMMODATION

BOOKING

Book well in advance for the peak tourist season in summer.

Lonely Planet (lonelyplanet.com/iceland/hotels) Find independent reviews, as well as recommendations on the best places to stay – and then book them online.

Bungalo (bungalo.com) Cottage rentals in Iceland. Great for groups.

Hey Iceland (heyiceland.is) Countryside accommodation and adventure tours.

Tjalda.is Provides an overview of campgrounds in Iceland. Pre-booking isn't necessary.

HOSTELS

Operating 29 hostels around the country, HI Iceland (hostel.is) is one way of stretching your accommodation budget further. The price for a dorm bed is about 3000kr to 5000kr per night and for a private room 10,000kr to 15,000kr. In addition to HI-operated hostels, there's also KEX Hostel in an old biscuit factory in Reykjavík, Hafnarstræti Hostel with capsule sleeping pods in Akureyri, and Kirkjubær guesthouse inside an old church in Stöðvarfjörður.

VAKINN
Quality

VAKINN
Vakinn offers certification for six accommodation categories and star ratings for hotels. Criteria focus on access, environment, security, shared areas, room facilities, cleanliness, service, education and staff training.

ESSENTIAL NUTS & BOLTS

POOL RULES

Everyone must shower and wash with soap without their swimsuits before entering the pool area (posters show the correct procedure).

SHOES OFF

Remove your shoes before entering someone's home. For other buildings, best practice is to check whether there's a shoe rack in the entryway.

SMOKING

It's forbidden to smoke inside public buildings; on rare occasions there are designated closed-off smoking areas.

FAST FACTS

Time Zone
GMT

Country Code
+354

Electricity
220V/50Hz

GOOD TO KNOW

Citizens from over 90 countries do not need a visa to enter Iceland (utl.is).

Stay on the right when driving, cycling and standing on escalators.

The legal drinking age is 20 years. Alcohol is sold at state-run stores called Vínbúð.

Travellers are entitled to VAT refund on purchases of more than 6000kr at a single point of sale.

Icelanders have a thing for liquorice in chocolate, which often suprises foreigners.

ACCESSIBLE TRAVEL

Hotels In several locations hotels have wheelchair-accessible rooms.

Dining Some restaurants offer accessible dining, especially in larger towns. Accessibility can be tricky in rural areas.

Public transport Public buses in Reykjavík are wheelchair accessible, but users have to enter and exit the bus on their own. Buses outside Reykjavík are not as accessible.

Sights The biggest natural attractions, like the Golden Circle, are wheelchair accessible. Consult with a travel agent specialising in accessible travel, such as Iceland Unlimited.

Apps Accessibility apps include TravAble. Also check out wheelmap.org.

Download Lonely Planet's free Accessible Travel Guide (http://lptravel.to/AccessibleTravel).

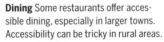

NO HONORIFICS
In Iceland everyone is on a first-name basis. Honorifics are hardly ever used.

GREETINGS
Shaking hands is the go-to greeting in Iceland. Friends (and very friendly strangers) hug. Kisses are for family.

BREASTFEEDING
Permitted in public and considered a natural thing. Mothers rarely cover up when feeding their babies.

FAMILY TRAVEL

Restaurants and cafes Usually welcome families and have high chairs and children's menus, sometimes colouring books and toys, and even a children's corner.

Sights and attractions Admission to museums, tours and swimming pools is usually free for children under six and sometimes for older children as well. Most places offer a lower rate for children up to a certain age.

Transport Child seats are available in taxis if you order them beforehand.

GEOTHERMAL WATER

Geothermal water is used for heating in most regions. Icelanders like their homes toasty and take long showers. However, in some parts of the country, especially the East and Westfjords, the water is heated with electricity and visitors are encouraged to keep their showers short.

RELIGION

Most Icelanders (80%) are members of the Lutheran State Church.
Another 5% are registered in other Christian denominations, including the Free Church of Iceland and the Roman Catholic Church.
Almost 5% of Icelanders practice *ásatrú*, the traditional Norse religion.

LGBTIQ+ TRAVELLERS

Iceland is progressive when it comes equality and non-discrimination, and Iceland is considered to be one of the most LGBTIQ+ friendly countries in the world

Reykjavík has the largest gay and lesbian scene. Reykjavík Pride in August is one of Iceland's most attended festivals. The Reykjavík Culture Walks app has a Queer Literature feature. For a night on the town, head to Kiki Queer Bar (p63).

Pink Iceland specialises in gay wedding, travel and event management.

For tips and news follow gayice.is and gayiceland.is.

ICELAND ESSENTIALS

LANGUAGE

Icelandic belongs to the Germanic language family, which includes German, English, Dutch and all the Scandinavian languages except Finnish. It's related to Old Norse, and retains the letters 'eth' *(ð)* and 'thorn' *(þ),* which also existed in Old English. Be aware, especially when you're trying to read bus timetables or road signs, that place names can be spelled in several different ways due to Icelandic grammar rules.

Most Icelanders speak English, so you'll have no problems if you don't know any Icelandic. However, any attempts to speak the local language will be much appreciated.

BASICS

Hello.	Halló.	*ha·loh*
Goodbye.	Bless.	*bles*
Yes.	Já.	*yow*
No.	Nei.	*nay*
Thank you	Takk./Takk fyrir.	*tak/tak fi·ri*
Excuse me.	Afsakið.	*af·sa·kidh*
Sorry.	Fyrirgefðu.	*fi·rir·gev·dhu*

What's your name?
Hvað heitir þú? *kvadh hay·tir thoo*

My name is ... Ég heiti .... *yekh hay·ti ...*

Do you speak English?
Talarðu ensku? *ta·lar dhoo ens·ku*

I don't understand.
Ég skil ekki. *yekh skil e·ki*

DIRECTIONS & NUMBERS

Where's the (hotel)?
Hvar er (hótelið)? *kvar er (hoh·te·lidh)*

Can you show me...?
Geturðu sýnt mér ...? *ge·tur·dhu seent myer...?*

Is this the ...	Er þetta ...	*er the·ta ...*
to...?	til...?	*til...*
boat	ferjan	*fer·yan*
bus	rútan	*roo·tan*

I'm lost.
Ég er villtur/villt. (m/f) *yekh er vil·tur/vilt*

1	einn	*aydn*	**6**	sex	*seks*
2	tveir	*tvayr*	**7**	sjö	*syeu*
3	þrír	*threer*	**8**	átta	*ow·ta*
4	fjórir	*fyoh·rir*	**9**	níu	*nee·u*
5	fimm	*fim*	**10**	tíu	*tee·u*

EMERGENCIES

Help!	Hjálp!	*hyowlp*
Call ...!	Hringdu á ...!	*hring·du ow ...*
a doctor	lækni	*laik·ni*
the police	lögregluna	*leukh·rekh·lu·na*

Where are the toilets?
Hvar er snyrtingin? *kvar er snir·tin·gin*

Index

000 Map pages

glamping 244
Golden Circle 37, 82-97, **84**
  accommodation 85, 96, 97
  drinking 85
  food 85, 96
  history 88-91
  money 85
  navigation 85
  planning 84
  travel seasons 85
  travel to Golden Circle 85
  travel within Golden Circle 85
golf 166
Grænavatn 113
Græni hatturinn 165
Grettir the Strong 187, 191
Grímsey 191, 203, 209
gyrfalcons 183, 184

H

Háleyjarbunga 113
Hallormsstaður Forest 13, 150-1
harlequin ducks 185
Heimaey 15, 114-15
Helgi Magri's Food Trail 161
Helgustaða Mine 147-8
helicopter tours 109
hiking
  Bæjarstaðarskógur Forest 138, 139
  Bláhnúkur Trail 127
  Borgarfjörður Eystri 152-3
  Brennisteinsalda Trail 127
  Fagradalsfjall 108-9
  Fálkafell 167
  Fimmvörðuháls Trail 121, 125
  Five-Summit Challenge 148
  Glerárdalur 167
  Hengifoss 151
  Hornbjarg 209

Hornstrandir 210-11, 212
Hraunsvatn 167
Kaldbakur 207
Kerling 161
Kristínartindar peaks 138-9
Landmannalaugar 126-7
Laugahringur Trail 127
Laugavegurinn 125, 127
Morsárjökull 136, 138
Naustahvilft 207
navigation 230
Reykjanes 109
safety 210, 221, 240
Skaftafell 134-7, 138-9
Skaftafellsjökull 139, 143
Snæfellsjökull 220-1
Sólheimajökull 129
Stórurð 13, 153
Súlur 167
Svalvogavegur 208
Svartifoss 135, 138
Svartifoss-Sjónarsker-Sel 139
Vatnajökull National Park 134-7, 138-9
Víknaslóðir Trail 153
West Iceland 230-1
Þingvellir National Park 87
Þórsmörk 124-5
history 6-7, 88-91, 187, 228-9
Höfn 35, 142-3
Hofsós 181
Hólmavík 41
Hornstrandir 210-11, 212
Hornvík 211
horses 192-3, 194-5, 232
  horse meat 56
  mythology 195
  riding 38, 79, 87, 95, 127, 161, 170, 193, 232
  round-ups 26, 38, 193

hostels 245
hot springs & geothermal pools 8-9, 23
  Blue Lagoon 102-3
  Brimketill 113
  Drangsnes 208
  East Iceland 154
  etiquette 9, 43, 103, 104-5, 246
  Forest Baths 197
  GeoSea Geothermal Sea Baths 183, 197
  Golden Circle 97
  Grettislaug 187
  Guðrúnarlaug 227
  Hrafnagil 161
  Kópavogslaug 73, 80
  Krossneslaug 208
  Landmannalaugar 127
  Laugarfell 197
  Reykjafjarðarlaug 209
  Reykjafjörður 207
  Reykjavík 80
  Secret Lagoon 84, 97
  Sky Lagoon 106-7
  South Coast 128-9
  Southwest Iceland 107
  Vesturbæjarlaug 77, 80
  Vök Baths 23, 145
  West Iceland 233
  Westfjords 214
Hrísey 191
Húsavíkurfjall 175
Hvammstangi 38, 181
Hvannadalshnúkur 135
Hveravellir Nature Reserve 39, 196

I

ice caves 29, 137, 232
ice cream 11, 105
icebergs 140-1

000 Map pages

ÞÓRGNÝR THORODDSEN

Þórgnýr was born and raised in the tourism industry in Reykjavík and always lived right in the heart of downtown. He has worked as a municipal politician, filmmaker, social worker and in the craft beer industry.

@ @thorgnyr

My favourite experience is bathing in the sea in Nauthólsvík and warming up in the tub afterwards with a coffee on the edge.

NAKGRUB/SHUTTERSTOCK ©

Skógafoss (p121)

THIS BOOK

Design development
Fergal Condon, Lauren Egan, Tina Garcia

Content development
Anne Mason

Cartography development
Wayne Murphy, Katerina Pavkova

Production development
Mario D'Arco, Sandie Kestell, Dan Moore, Virginia Moreno, Juan Winata

Series development leadership
Liz Heynes, Darren O'Connell, Piers Pickard, Chris Zeiher

Commissioning Editor
Daniel Bolger

Product Editor
Lauren O'Connell

Book Designer
Ania Bartoszek

Cartographer
Mark Griffiths, Rachel Imeson

Assisting Editors
Gabrielle Stefanos, Simon Williamson

Cover Researcher
Lauren Egan

Thanks Kristopher Clifford, Karen Henderson, Katherine Marsh, Juzar Valiji

Our Writers

ZOË ROBERT

Based in Reykjavík, Zoë has covered Iceland for publications including Reuters, CNN, Icelandair's *Stopover* magazine, the Reykjavík Grapevine and Iceland Review, where she was also managing editor. She has lived in various places but calls Iceland home.

My favourite experience is a secluded summer hike followed by a splash in the cool sea or nearby lake or river. Also enjoyed in the cooler months.

EYGLÓ SVALA ARNARSDÓTTIR

Akureyri-native Eygló has written for and edited various travel publications, including *Iceland Review*, and currently works at an advertising agency.

My favourite experience is horse trekking in the Icelandic highlands.

EGILL BJARNASON

Born in Reykjavík; Egill reports on Iceland for The Associated Press and is the author of *How Iceland Changed the World: The Big History of a Small Island*, published by Penguin Books in 2021.

@ @egilssaga

My favourite experience is whale watching in the northern Skjálfandi Bay.

JEANNIE RILEY

Jeannie was born in the United States and has been living in Iceland since 2015. She currently runs the travel planning website called Iceland with a View.

@ @icelandwithaview

My favourite experience is road tripping around Iceland discovering new places and experiencing Iceland's neverending gorgeous landscapes.